1997

A Culture for Academic Excell
Implementing the Quality Principles in
Higher Education

Jann E. Freed, Marie R. Klugman, and Jonathan D. Fife

ASHE-ERIC Higher Education Report, Vol. 25, No. 1

Prepared by

Clearinghouse on Higher Education
The George Washington University

In cooperation with

Association for the Study
of Higher Education

Published by

The
George
Washington
University
WASHINGTON DC

Graduate School of Education and Human Development
The George Washington University

Jonathan D. Fife, Series Editor

Cite as

Freed, Jann E., Marie R. Klugman, and Jonathan D. Fife. 1997. *A Culture for Academic Excellence: Implementing the Quality Principles in Higher Education.* ASHE-ERIC Higher Education Report, Vol. 25, No. 1. Washington, D.C.: The George Washington University, Graduate School of Education and Human Development.

Library of Congress Catalog Card Number 96-79499
ISSN 0884-0040
ISBN 1-878-380-73-7

Managing Editor: Lynne J. Scott
Manuscript Editor: Barbara Fishel/Editech
Cover Design by Michael David Brown, Inc., The Red Door Gallery, Rockport, ME

The ERIC Clearinghouse on Higher Education invites individuals to submit proposals for writing monographs for the *ASHE-ERIC Higher Education Report* series. Proposals must include:
1. A detailed manuscript proposal of not more than five pages.
2. A chapter-by-chapter outline.
3. A 75-word summary to be used by several review committees for the initial screening and rating of each proposal.
4. A vita and a writing sample.

ERIC Clearinghouse on Higher Education
Graduate School of Education and Human Development
The George Washington University
One Dupont Circle, Suite 630
Washington, DC 20036-1183

The mission of the ERIC system is to improve American education by increasing and facilitating the use of educational research and information on practice in the activities of learning, teaching, educational decision making, and research, wherever and whenever these activities take place.

This publication was prepared partially with funding from the Office of Education Research and Improvement, U.S. Department of Education, under contract no. ED RR-93-002008. The opinions expressed in this report do not necessarily reflect the positions or policies of OERI or the Department.

EXECUTIVE SUMMARY

Striving for high quality is not a new strategy for higher
education institutions, which have always held academic
excellence and high quality as the highest goals. Achieving
these goals was easier, however, in a time of abundant resources and favorable demographics. But the environment
has changed. Institutions face decreasing enrollments and
revenues at the same time costs and competition for students are increasing.

Many institutions have attempted to become more competitive by improving the quality or distinctiveness of their
academic and administrative areas. In this search for excellence, many new techniques, such as management or teaching by objectives, strategic planning, assessment, value-
added measurement, and reengineering have been tried
with only limited success. Many higher education institutions
have now begun to realize that these methods achieved only
partial success because they were only part of a larger set of
quality principles. Individually, these principles are not new
or unique, but implemented as a total system, they are a
new philosophical way of thinking about how institutions
operate. When they are implemented as a system, the quality principles create a culture for academic excellence.

What Is Meant by "Quality Principles"?

The quality principles are a management approach for making higher education institutions more effective and for creating an improved place to obtain a degree and a more en-
joyable workplace. The principles were conceptualized and
documented by such authorities as W. Edwards Deming,
Joseph M. Juran, and Philip B. Crosby, and they have been
widely implemented in corporate America under the name
of total quality management. The literature contains abundant articles indicating that the quality principles are proven
ways of improving organizations' effectiveness and efficiency, and numerous companies across a variety of industries—among them Motorola, Ford, Xerox, and FedEx—have
benefited from implementing the quality principles. And
now, as evidenced by the American Association for Higher
Education's Continuous Quality Improvement Project, many
higher education institutions are demonstrating the benefits
of the quality principles for higher education (American
Association 1994).

What Are the Quality Principles?

Taken together, the quality principles are *a personal philosophy and an organizational culture that uses scientific measurement of outcomes, systematic management techniques, and collaboration to achieve an institution's mission.* Essentially, the quality principles change the culture of higher education institutions.

A review of the literature on quality improvement reveals eight quality principles. One of the principles, leadership, is needed early in the quality journey to create a quality culture and is vital later in the journey to support quality improvement. The quality principles:

- Are *vision, mission, and outcomes driven.* The more clearly defined an institution's sense of purpose and desired results, the more impact it has on all its stakeholders.
- Are *systems dependent.* Almost all action in an organization affects some other part of the organization. Understanding the relationships and dependencies of the parts or systems greatly improves decision making.
- Require *leadership* that creates a quality culture. If the quality principles are to become an integral part of an organization's way of doing business, leadership throughout the organization must believe these principle are fundamental to the organization's basic values and success.
- Display *systematic individual development.* Because the requirements and skills needed to do every job in an institution change continuously, efforts are necessary to ensure that everyone has a specific plan for continuously developing his or her interpersonal and career skills to fit the institution's changing needs.
- Employ *decisions based on fact.* Most problems recur because no one took the time to define the problem clearly, collect data to identify the ultimate cause of the problem, and then gradually implement solutions until the most effective one is found. The more problem solving is based on in-depth fact-finding, the greater the likelihood of long-term, effective decision making.
- *Delegate decision making.* Although an organization's overall direction or vision is most effectively set at the top, the people who have the most knowledge about the day-to-day implementation of this vision are those doing the work. When they continuously update their skills and

receive appropriate data, the people on the front line are the ones best equipped to make day-to-day decisions.

- Ensure *collaboration*. If people are to work together effectively, information, ideas, and a sense of a common purpose must be shared. The greater the collaboration and teamwork among individuals and interdependent units, the more effective the institution.
- *Plan for change.* The physical, technological, demographic, and intellectual environment of higher education is increasingly changing. The more an institution develops a culture that encourages and anticipates change, the more likely it will be capable of meeting the demands of change.
- Require *supportive leaders*. If the quality principles are to successfully become part of an organization's culture, leaders must understand the interdependency of the principles and constantly work to see that adequate resources and systems are available to implement them effectively.

What Makes the Quality Principles Different?

The quality principles are interrelated and interdependent, and they need to be implemented as a system, driven by the institution's vision and mission. That vision and mission are defined by the needs and expectations of those the institution was created to benefit—its stakeholders. For higher education institutions, stakeholders include faculty, students, administrators, parents, employers, the research community, alumni, the local community, and society in general. As stakeholders' expectations change, so does the institution's vision and mission. The power of the principles comes from the synergy of the whole system, fundamentally linking the mission to measurable outcomes.

How Can the Quality Principles Work In Higher Education Institutions?

The quality principles essentially are compatible with the values of higher education, but often parts of an individual institution's culture must change to support the principles. Most institutions have missions, but most are not accustomed to measuring the outcomes of their processes. Traditionally, constituencies in higher education institutions act independently rather than interdependently. Leaders are usually not trained in the tools and techniques used to improve systems and processes. Developing management skills and knowledge is not the norm in higher education. Professional development is more often discipline- and person-specific rather than oriented toward developing members who can collectively improve institutional processes. Although data are collected for a variety of purposes in directing higher education institutions, the quality principles emphasize the *systematic* collection of data to be used in making academic and administrative decisions. Committees in academe are common, but collaborating and working as teams for common purposes are not.

If the culture is to change, members must shift their thinking about how work is done. When an institution's traditional way of doing something changes—moving from passive to active learning or from autocratic to collaborative leadership, for example—the paradigm shifts, because members begin to ask different questions in search of new answers to the same old problems. They embrace change as a positive value in the culture because continuous improvement is based on continuous change. People are trained to feel comfortable with change and not fear becoming involved in efforts to improve the institution. Planning for change is an attitude to be cultivated by the leaders of an institution. Leaders are essential in creating a quality culture, and they play a significant role in ensuring that the necessary resources are available to support quality initiatives. The holistic implementation of the quality principles creates a culture for academic excellence.

CONTENTS

TABLES

FIGURES

FOREWORD

Years ago, as a newly minted marketing professor, I read W. Edwards Deming's *Out of the Crisis*. My knowledge of "quality" at the time extended not much farther than Ford's making air bags standard on its new models. Understandably, I was intrigued by the richness of Deming's ideas. His prescriptions struck a responsive chord in me, and I began to explore and read more broadly. Before long, I started weaving quality principles into lectures and began focusing projects for my students on how customers' requirements could drive the redesign of processes.

My career path took a sidestep when I accepted an administrative position at my university; my understanding of quality principles and practices took an upswing when I quietly began applying my newfound knowledge to some lingering administrative problems. Still, years later, after studying, teaching, and "doing" quality, I often felt uneasy with my own knowledge. The feeling was akin to leaving for a long trip and thinking I forgot something. Something was missing. But what?

One day I found my answer. I had bought a pair of expensive glasses. After several months of looking appropriately designer-esque, I went to punctuate a critical point in a lecture and, wiping off my glasses, left a nosepiece steadfastly perched on my face. I went back to the store—a national chain—and explained my problem. The store displayed a large sign proclaiming its single-minded devotion to its customers, and so I was not surprised to find a young clerk eager to help. She set off to fix the problem. In a flash, she was back, having inserted a larger screw into the straying nosepiece and frame.

Unfortunately, within a few weeks the scenario repeated itself: another dramatic point, the failure of another nosepiece. I returned to the store. This time was different, however. As the clerk turned away in search of another screw, these words escaped my mouth: "Are you recording this anywhere?" I was unconscious of having formed the thought before I spoke. It was a mental reflex. Nonetheless, the effect was similar to the one that occurs when the seal of a vacuum is broken. All my readings and experiences, all my feelings of apprehension and angst, came rushing together. For my inquiry—unstudied and unsolicited—meant only one thing: I finally got it. Things suddenly made sense to me, not just intellectually, but also personally. I understood—in my gut.

The explanation is really quite simple. "Are you recording this anywhere?" was a manifestation of my unconscious struggle with several other questions: "Do you have a quality system in place?" and "Are you measuring the right things?" As it was, "quality" to this company was having a nice sign, showing concern and heartfelt remorse when a problem presented itself, finding and fixing the problem, and sending the customer off with a cheery "thank you." But the chain and the manufacturer did not work together to *prevent* problems from happening. If they had, a system would have been in place to gather data, analyze it, and provide feedback to the manufacturer in an effort to continuously improve the product. To do that, the company needed to measure the right things—and it obviously was not.

What I realize now is that my level of discomfort rose in direct proportion to my knowledge. I had competence but little understanding; I had know-how but little know-why. Like an extended family scattered across the country, my knowledge had been extended but lacked wholeness. My epiphany was the family reunion. It was a gathering of isolated ideas and fragmented experiences; it was a comforting and spiritual feeling; it was an antidote to my personal Diaspora.

The strength of *A Culture for Academic Excellence: Implementing the Quality Principles in Higher Education* is its feeling of a family reunion. Jann Freed, Marie Klugman, and Jonathan Fife pull together a broad array of ideas and answer a slew of nagging questions. Their distress at seeing so much of what quality principles and practices have to offer being squandered is evident throughout the manuscript. It covers the mimicked catchphrases ("what gets measured gets done"), wrong-headed beliefs ("it's fine for the administrators and staff but not for the faculty"), draining debates ("students are not customers"), and gaffs in implementation, such as an early focus on extensive training in the tools of quality improvement. It also covers the seemingly endless squabbles over the commercialization of higher education that goes round and round as if the combatants were running with one shoe nailed to the floor.

The authors manage to blend such disharmonies with hard-edged research and a splendid mix of cross-disciplinary concepts. They strike a harmonizing chord that leads the reader in an important direction: from pieces toward a whole, from fragmentation toward integration. They provide the conceptual and organizational glue to move from chaos toward order, from knowledge toward one's own personal nosepiece-like epiphany.

A Culture for Academic Excellence is indeed a direction well worth taking.

Daniel T. Seymour
The Claremont Colleges, California

Dr. Seymour is author of *On Q: Causing Quality in Higher Education* (1992) and *Higher Performancing Colleges: The Malcolm Baldrige National Quality Awards as a Framework for Improving Higher Education* (1996).

ACKNOWLEDGMENTS

The authors would like to thank Central College, Drake University, and The George Washington University for their financial assistance and for their continuing support of the authors' research. We also appreciate the input of Steve Brigham and Daniel Seymour in design of the survey instrument that underlies this report, Campus Services at Central College for its help in typesetting, printing, and mailing the survey, and Randa Van Dyk, graphic artist at Central College, for her work on the report's figures and tables.

Finally, we are particularly grateful for the patience and understanding of our families throughout this project.

INTRODUCTION

Within our colleges and our faculties of arts and sciences, we need to persuade the public—but most of all ourselves—that we do make the quality of education a priority second to none (Bok 1992, p. 19).

Quality is not a new concept in higher education. Institutions have always striven for academic excellence and high quality. What is new is the rapidly changing environment in which institutions operate and the changing public and professional perception of what defines a quality institution.

Even though articles about the improvement of quality are becoming increasingly abundant in the literature, the principles used to define a quality organization and how those principles support the historic values of higher education must be better understood. Observers must also realize that the current culture of higher education is often at odds with these historic values and therefore must be changed. The purpose of this monograph is to review comprehensively the quality principles in higher education and to explain that when used holistically and systematically, the quality principles create a culture for academic excellence.

. . . the quality principles . . . when used holistically and systematically . . . create a culture for academic excellence.

The Context for Quality Principles in Higher Education

The history of American higher education since 1940 delineates a trend of responding to serious challenges in demographics, economics, and changing social values. For at least two decades after World War II, enrollments increased, revenues rose, and new programs were created. Competition was limited as few corporations offered degree programs and accreditation was restricted to colleges and universities, and the availability of federal dollars offset college costs (Whetten and Cameron 1985). At the same time, quality was based on institutional reputation, which was often a reflection of admission test scores, size of endowment, and percentage of Ph.D.s on the faculty.

The situation changed in the 1970s and 1980s: Federal funds were reduced, the value of a college degree was questioned, corporations began offering courses and degrees, and shifting demographics led to declining enrollments of traditional students. Accompanying these changes were rising tuition and the public's demand for more accountability and increased productivity (Fincher 1991).

A disturbing and dangerous mismatch exists between what American society needs of higher education and what it is receiving. Nowhere is the mismatch more dangerous than in the quality of undergraduate preparation provided on many campuses. The American imperative for the 21st century is that society must hold higher education to much higher expectations or risk national decline (Wingspread 1993, p. 1).

Concurrently, college enrollments have become increasingly competitive, to the point where an understanding of how to market the institution is of the highest priority. Parents and students "shop" for the institution that will best meet their needs, often based on their perceptions of the quality of the institution and the associated costs of attending. They search for the best value for the dollars they spend, and the value is often situational. Higher education is accustomed to thinking of value in terms of low cost or exclusivity —thinking that is not appropriate for the existing external environment (Dehne 1995). The concept of value changes, depending on the "shopping" and the goals. Therefore, institutions need to understand better how students select institutions. They need to offer "programs, opportunities, and a 'product' students value" (p. 13).

With the public's concern about the value of higher education and educational outcomes, the definition of quality is changing. The traditional concept of quality in higher education had an internal focus emphasizing product and service. Technical experts defined the criteria and assessed the product. The current shift is toward an external focus emphasizing stakeholders'* expectations. Stakeholders define quality and evaluate the outcomes (Ruben 1995a).

Higher education traditionally has evaluated itself in terms of inputs and resources rather than outcomes and amount of value added. Measurements of resources (admission test scores, size of endowment, library collections, Ph.D.s on the faculty, for example) determined quality, but the public is

---

*"Stakeholder" is used throughout this report to refer to all those an institution was created to benefit. It includes faculty, students, administrators, parents, employers, the research community, alumni, the local community, and society in general.

increasingly concerned about institutional performance and stakeholders' satisfaction (Balderston 1995, pp. 279–301; Seymour 1993b).

Public opinion, as reflected in newspapers and magazines, indicates the loss of public trust largely because of a lack of evidence of the impact of higher education institutions. The Task Force on College Quality of the National Governors Association has noted the public's increasing skepticism about the value of higher education to society and questions the role most institutions play:

> *The public has the right to know what it is getting for its expenditure of tax resources; the public has a right to know and understand the quality of undergraduate education that young people receive from publicly funded colleges and universities. They have a right to know that their resources are being wisely invested and committed. . . . Public policy makers, taxpayers, students, and parents should expect colleges and universities to fulfill their promises. To assure accountability, postsecondary institutions must assess [students'] learning and ability, [programs'] effectiveness, and [institutions'] accomplishment of [their] mission* (Mayhew, Ford, and Hubbard 1990, p. 11).

"There is a major erosion of confidence in the leadership and the quality of higher education in the country. Respect for colleges and universities is gravely in danger" (Cornesky, McCool, Byrnes, and Weber 1991, p. 1). Moreover, "there seems to be a widespread public questioning of the value of our educational institutions, particularly whether they are worth all we are paying for them and skepticism that they are administered wisely and prudently" (Chaffee and Seymour 1991, p. 14). Critics of higher education charge that the decline of higher education institutions has had a negative impact on numerous stakeholders: on students, by offering diluted courses taught by mediocre teachers; on parents, who are often paying for higher college costs; on American businesses, which are hiring unprepared graduates; on American society, which indirectly is funding research and supporting people employed in nonprofit organizations (Anderson 1992; McPherson, Schapiro, and Winston 1993; Smith 1990; Sykes 1988; Weinstein 1993; Wilshire 1990).

One indication of how the public feels is the national index of public support, an index of the revenue raised for the education of students relative to the income of taxpayers, adjusted for the number of students and the number of people in the population. The index was 21.8 in 1992, the lowest level since 1930 (U.S. Dept. of Education 1995). In 1990, the rate of increase in state support for higher education dropped to a 30-year low, while real federal funding for university research decreased 18 percent from 1967 to 1990. As these numbers indicate, it will be difficult for public institutions to compete with other public priorities because of declining public support.

Moreover, most independent colleges and universities will find their survival threatened by rising costs in all facets of the institution as they struggle to recruit students (Bonser 1992). Even as public support declines, college costs continue to rise for all types of institutions. Between 1980 and 1993, college costs rose rapidly in both public and private institutions. Tuition at public and private institutions continues to rise faster than the rate of inflation, although more slowly than in the 1980s. Between 1980 and 1993, tuition, room, and board at public institutions increased from 10 percent to 14 percent of median family income. At private institutions, that percent rose every year between 1979 and 1993, from 23 percent to 41 percent of median family income. From 1993 through 1996, tuition costs at public and private universities rose 6 percent each year, while inflation was below 3 percent (Kelly 1996). As costs continue to rise, prospective students and their parents question the value of a college education relative to costs. According to a 1993 study on issues related to college funding, 45 percent of parents and 36 percent of students believe a college education costs more than it is worth (Dehne 1995).

To make the situation even worse, the average GRE (Graduate Record Examination) verbal score has not recovered from the decline of the 1960s, 1970s, and early 1980s; in 1993, the score was 49 points below the average score in 1965 (U.S. Dept. of Education 1995). The increasing costs of attending an institution, combined with the poorer performance of graduates on standardized tests, has led to a growing dissatisfaction with higher education in America.

Based on these statistics, there is room for improvement in higher education. College officials echo their counterparts in business and industry. Conversations on campus are not about new courses or interdisciplinary majors, but about program cutbacks and operating efficiency. Because institutions are no longer operating in a period of growth, "higher education will have to live with relatively less" (Levine 1990, p. 4).

All indicators point to a need for a major change in higher education, making quality based on amount of value added and educational outcomes a priority. Given the traditions of the past, it is easy to think of higher education institutions as indispensable and lasting forever. But the challenges currently faced demand that institutions respond, adapt, and be proactive. When institutions fail to meet the needs and expectations of society, a period of extreme turmoil occurs first, after which society begins to back away and search for alternative ways of accomplishing the goals, followed by indifference and funding cuts as new organizations begin to satisfy existing needs (Marchese 1994).

Many argue that higher education has become less relevant to society ("Transatlantic Dialogue" 1993). Bill Massy, director of the Stanford Institute for Higher Education Research, says that "many people continue to doubt that higher education has generated as much value for the money as possible" (*Chronicle* 1994, p. 1). According to its president, Motorola is not spending money on education and training because it wants to, but because the higher education system is not working for it. The company is not satisfied with the outcomes of the educational system (Marchese 1994). Higher education institutions are being challenged from all directions: students, state legislatures, parents, employers, and alumni (Boyer 1994; Kerr 1990; "To Dance" 1994).

"Quality improvement" is one way that some institutions are using to address these challenges. The purpose of this monograph is to review the quality principles in higher education and explain how they create a culture that supports the improvement of quality. Individually, the principles are familiar, but this report explains how the principles must be used together, systematically and holistically, for continuous improvement of the institutional culture.

Historical Practices as Obstacles
To Continuous Improvement

Historically, institutions are based on long-standing traditions and practices, with the traditions based on an accumulation of consistently acted-out values. For example, such traditions include the 15-week semester system, the three-credit-per-semester course, the assessment of students' learning through final exams, and faculty development based on sabbaticals every seven years. The norm in higher education is to measure success by inputs rather than overall outcomes and by processes that tend to remain constant over time.

But these traditional practices and processes are obstacles to continuous improvement. These traditions have remained fairly consistent at a time when the external environment is inconsistent and changing. Institutions have not responded to these demands in a way that would position them positively for the changes taking place. Rather than anticipating the changes and adapting to them, institutions have looked for a new approach and made changes in a piecemeal fashion without considering the impact on the whole system. The traditions are so strong that what has been most desirable is any action that would make the pressure for change disappear yet keep the status quo intact.

The issues that now face higher education, however, are no longer solved by small, disconnected bandages applied in the hope of making it through the next year. These challenges have forced institutions to examine their inherent quality and to consider the publics they serve. "I know of no industry that has experienced this juxtaposition of financial pressures and technological progress that has not gone through fundamental change," says Massy (*Chronicle* 1994, p. 2). The wake-up call has sounded for many institutions.

In business and industry, the driving forces of the movement toward continuous quality improvement include increasing competition, both domestic and international, changing demands from customers, advances in technology, and a realization that the quality principles are simply "good business." Likewise, higher education institutions are experiencing pressure from state agencies and requirements from accreditation bodies and government units to operate more efficiently and effectively—in the face of shrinking resources and a smaller pool of students.

Although strong external reasons exist for institutions to improve quality, academe has been slow to adopt the quality principles. Academicians tend to resist quality initiatives, because they perceive the effort as coming from the business sector and because they are unaware of how the quality principles can support academic values. This situation is a consequence of academic values and program improvement not being a regular part of faculty training or departmental conversation and business—which in turn is a consequence of the topics not being part of a department chair's agenda.

The need for greater preparation and training of chairs is a strong theme in the literature concerning the roles and responsibilities of department chairs in various types of institutions (Seagren, Creswell, and Wheeler 1993). When faculty are not trained, they do not have the opportunity to discuss the principles as they relate to higher education. When academic leaders, such as department chairs, are not educated in the quality principles, faculty are not encouraged to implement the principles and practices. For these reasons, most efforts to implement the quality principles have been focused on improving administrative operations and units like the physical plant, the registrar's office, admissions, and students affairs—areas where the quality movement can be easily legislated (Chaffee and Sherr 1992; Hansen 1993; Seymour and Collett 1991).

A concern for quality is not new in higher education: Colleges and universities have always been engaged in the pursuit of excellence. What is new is the changing definition of quality—a change from focusing on quality teaching to quality learning. Institutions are focusing on effectiveness and efficiency by improving processes to decrease costs while maintaining and improving quality. Out of the public and professional dialogue on higher education are emerging fundamental questions about the purpose, value, competitiveness, effectiveness, efficiency, and confidence in the future of higher education (Ruben 1995a).

Some states have instituted quality awards for which profit and not-for-profit organizations compete. Receiving such an award can influence state funding and have a positive impact on the public's perception of the organization. The Malcolm Baldrige National Quality Award program, for example, has developed criteria for higher education institutions to encourage them to instigate quality initiatives. These criteria focus on how well institutions, by using the quality principles, are meeting the expectations of their stakeholders. Based on the Baldrige award criteria, the driving forces in the external environment are redefining quality in higher education (Seymour 1996).

The current environment challenging business and industry is the same environment challenging higher education institutions. Colleges and universities, like other organizations, produce goods or services to satisfy a particular set of needs. When organizations achieve success and stability, the structures, systems, policies, practices, and leadership styles associated with those accomplishments are accepted and institutionalized. It is also true of the culture that supports and reinforces these patterns. In the short term, these relationships may lead to success (Ruben 1995a). In the long term, these "patterns that lead to success can lead to rigidity, insulation, lack of innovation, and gradual distancing from the needs of the marketplace and expectations of consumers" (p. 3). Competition, economics, technology, demographics, and the political and legal environment are changing at an ever-increasing rate, and organizations need to be able to adapt to these changes while meeting the expectations of consumers. "Unless new ways of thinking and working and new cultures to support these changes are developed, the prognosis for vitality is poor" (p. 3).

Although new cultures are needed to support these changes, the changes should be gradual and compatible with the current culture. The current institutional vision, mission, and outcomes should be respected at the same time a culture is created that supports new thoughts, new behaviors, and new actions. When current stakeholders are involved in developing the vision, mission, and outcomes, the culture is able to gradually change at the same time it respects the culture of the past.

Organizations are moving from "hierarchical, function-based structures to horizontal, integrated workplaces organized around empowered individuals and self-directed work teams as the means to achieve sustainable process changes" (Graham and LeBaron 1994, p. xv). Instead of managing by controlling information, leaders manage by exchanging information. So that people can collaborate, people who are involved in a process are brought together to improve the process. With collaboration, the thinking shifts from "It's not my job" to "How are we going to do this?"

Simpler, flatter, better-integrated organizations [that] facilitate cross-functional and cross-divisional collaboration, coordination, and teamwork are seen as means for addressing . . . [consumers'] expectations, aligning individuals and functional units with the organization's mission, [and] improving organizational quality overall (Ruben 1995a, p. 18).

Members are rewarded for developing multiple skills and working together effectively rather than for specialization and individualism. In the traditional hierarchy where politics, status, and egos dominated, the culture that supports the improvement of quality is based on trustworthiness, equality, and creativity (Byrne 1993; Kilmann, Covin, and Associates 1988).

Another characteristic of the changes taking place is the integration of stakeholders' expectations. The primary motivation for implementing the quality principles is to have greater assurance that the organization will achieve its vision and mission. Under the quality principles, an organization's vision and mission are defined by stakeholders' expectations, which translates into stakeholders' greater involvement in the long-range planning of the organization. Stakeholders should be included as team members when their perspectives are relevant to the decisions being made so that their needs are recognized and understood. These changes involve developing new skills for building trust, providing flexibility and adaptability, and working in teams. Including stakeholders' expectations in the planning process also means the sharing of power, information, and rewards. And it means a greater sharing of responsibility for the success of the organization. Therefore, continuous education and training are also necessary if employees are to acquire the necessary skills.

Creating a culture for academic excellence by implementing the quality principles will not be easy for higher education institutions, as the strong historical traditions in higher education make any kind of change extremely difficult. When demographic trends pointed to an increasing pool of students, many colleges and universities created infrastructures, including buildings and facilities, on the assumption that the student population would increase and financial and human resources would grow. They constructed buildings, hired people, and granted tenure in a time of rapid growth. But such decisions and academic practices tend to inhibit change, because buildings and tenured positions are fairly permanent and do not allow for flexibility. And because higher education historically has evaluated itself on inputs rather than outcomes, academic quality and reputation have often been based on level of resources (for example, endowments, size of the library, number of faculty with doctorates)—a radically different approach from the organizations driven by quality principles that measure quality according to an institution's performance (Dehne 1995; Seymour 1993b).

The Need for Change

The evidence that business as usual is no longer acceptable can be seen in a number of books severely critical of the education process (Anderson 1992; Smith 1990; Sykes 1988; Weinstein 1993; Wilshire 1990) and of cost issues (Levine 1990). "We might be *for* quality, but in many eyes we do not *do* quality" (Chaffee and Sherr 1992, p. 1).

> *Academic life in America today exists in a world with too many schools and too few students, too many fixed costs and too few discretionary dollars, too many competitors and too few supporters. In such a world, survival does belong to the fittest, which will be those institutions imbued with a passion for quality that extends to every member of the community, faculty included* (Hull 1992, p. 227).

Institutions are operating in a time when the public demands a clear purpose for existence. Institutions must demonstrate their value to individuals and society as a whole, collecting evidence to support their value. People within the institution must understand their connection to the accomplishment of the institution's mission and goals. Most institutions are achieving their overall vision and mission, but how well they weather the challenges for greater accountability will be based on their clarifying their purpose and on people working together to clearly demonstrate that the programs being provided bring value to the people they serve (Bok 1992).

The Quality Principles

A basic premise of the quality principles is that they are a fundamental and philosophical culture value. Institutions that treat the quality principles as an incremental management technique that can be called on from time to time rather than an immutable organizational culture value are less able to make them work and therefore are not able to incorporate them into the fabric of the institution. It is not enough to implement a few of the principles, because each principle draws its strength from and is interdependent with the other principles. A thorough knowledge of how each principle functions and of the relationships among the principles is necessary before institutions can make the quality principles part of their culture. By viewing the quality principles holistically, this report analyzes continuous improvement in higher education from a different perspective than the past.

This report defines eight quality principles, one of which, leadership, has two parts. These quality principles:

A basic premise of the quality principles is that they are a fundamental and philosophical culture value.

- Are *vision, mission, and outcomes driven;* that is, the organization has a clear sense of direction and focus defined by its stakeholders.
- Are *systems dependent;* that is, all actions are part of interactive and interdependent processes or systems, and a change in one part of the institution has an impact on the other parts.
- Create a *leadership* that understands that the quality principles are an integral part of the organization's culture and a fundamental philosophy of doing business.
- Display *systematic individual development;* that is, knowledge and skills of all members are continuously updated through education, training, and career planning.
- Employ *decisions based on fact;* that is, the long-range success of a decision depends on the degree to which appropriate information has been gathered and considered.
- *Delegate decision making;* that is, people who are involved in the day-to-day performance of an operation have the best knowledge of that operation and therefore should be involved in making decisions affecting that operation.
- Ensure *collaboration;* that is, people who have a stake in an organization's outcomes should work together to define the processes that creates the outcomes.
- *Plan for change* (the foundation for continuous quality improvement, reengineering, and reassessment of assumptions); that is, because change is inevitable, it should be

embraced and planning for change should be a daily priority.

- Require *supportive leaders;* that is, having accepted the quality principles as an integral part of institutional culture, leaders must support this culture by designing systems and making the necessary resources available to implement the quality principles.

This definition of the quality principles includes two aspects of leadership: (1) leaders who *create* the quality culture and (2) leaders who *support* the quality culture. It is the principle of leadership that perpetuates the quality improvement system and enables the other principles to come full circle, reinforcing the underlying premise that the principles need to be implemented as a system if they are to become operationalized within an institution. These eight principles are guidelines for human behavior. Organizations change when individuals change, so individuals must change. The quality principles* facilitate change.

The Quality Principles and a Change in Culture
Implementing the quality principles may be a significant change in culture for higher education. For example, institutional missions are often vague, and it is often difficult to distinguish one institution's mission statement from another's. Institutions are not accustomed to measuring the outcomes of their processes; they typically do not systematically measure whether students leave with higher-level skills than when they entered the institution. The assumption is that value has been added, but this assumption traditionally has not been validated. Assessing their practices and measuring the amount of value added are only recent priorities for many higher education institutions. Institutions historically have operated as separate entities, with faculty, administrators, and staff acting as independent contractors working in isolation instead of working together. Viewing institutions as systems

---

*At this point, it is important to distinguish between a practice and a principle. A practice works in one situation and not necessarily in another, while principles are fundamental truths that have universal application. When truths are internalized into personal habits, people are empowered to create a variety of practices to address different situations. Therefore, principles are guidelines for human behavior because they have enduring, permanent value (Covey 1989). Together, these eight principles shape the institution by operating as a continuous system.

of interdependent parts, each contributing to achievement of the mission, is not the norm in higher education.

Moreover, institutions have traditionally operated without a focus on stakeholders' expectations. Faculty decided what was considered appropriate for the curriculum and how it was to be taught. Although establishment of the land-grant colleges and creation of comprehensive community colleges are examples of the public's dissatisfaction with the lack of faculty responsiveness to stakeholders' needs, faculty continue to have total say over content of the curriculum. And because of this inward focus on the curriculum, institutions have existed without a strong sense of the need to consider the expectations of those served and therefore made little effort to collect data about stakeholders' expectations. On the whole, the culture of higher education has had leaders making decisions based on intuition and personal or "professional" experience instead of data. Traditionally, "strong, charismatic" leaders have been rewarded for making decisions independently, often based on little data (Fisher 1984). Without measurement of institutional processes and outcomes, often no short-term way exists of knowing the effectiveness of these decisions and this form of leadership thus often continues until it becomes evident that it is time for new leadership.

In a culture that supports quality improvement, vision and mission statements are revisited regularly to continually anchor institutional outcomes. Involving current stakeholders in developing these statements ensures that their input is included in defining and redefining the institution. The quality principles are not a top-down approach, but an inclusive approach in which every voice has an opportunity to be heard.

Leaders empower individuals and teams by sharing information and involving them in making decisions. This involvement makes the mission come alive, helps to align members to a shared vision, and creates ownership for the process and outcomes. Decisions are based on the input of the people most affected by the decisions. But leaders must also ensure that everyone has the appropriate skills and knowledge to be successful in his or her job. Thus, people must be continuously trained and educated. Traditionally, professional development has been related to a specific discipline and has occurred independently or sporadically. A quality culture emphasizes that learning is a continuous process, and to continuously educate members on a variety of topics, systematic individual development becomes a part of the overall system.

The quality principles are fundamentally comparable to the basic values of higher education but require a gradual culture change to ensure that the values are part of an institution's daily existence.

Higher Education Institutions' Adoption Of the Quality Principles

Several higher education authors support the concept of an educational system based on the quality principles (see, e.g., Chaffee and Sherr 1992; Marchese 1993; Ruben 1995a, 1995b; Seymour 1992, 1993a, 1996; Seymour and Collett 1991), advocating institutions' adoption of the philosophy and tools of quality as a better way to operate higher education institutions. The quality movement cannot be dismissed as another management fad (Pfeffer 1995; Seymour 1992). It is too well grounded in a scientific approach to problem solving, and it has been tested in numerous organizations in a variety of industries over a period of more than three decades.

A number of higher education institutions have begun to adopt the quality principles and to define quality according to stakeholders' expectations and educational outcomes (Miller 1991; Seymour 1992; Sherr and Teeter 1991; Spanbauer 1992). Table 1 lists institutions that were among the first to consciously implement the quality principles.

Research indicates organizations that use quality practices are more successful than those that follow traditional models. Greater revenues, stakeholders' increased satisfaction, lower costs, higher productivity, and superior services are often outcomes of institutions using quality principles (Melissaratos and Arendt 1992).* Moreover, certain high-performing colleges have used the Malcolm Baldrige

---

*Further support for the success of the quality approach comes from a study of Baldrige winners' common stock. For two consecutive years (1995 and 1996), the National Institute of Standards and Technology's study of stock investments found that quality management resulted in impressive returns. When NIST "invested" a hypothetical sum of money in the Standard & Poor's 500 and in each of the publicly traded companies (five whole companies and nine parent companies of subsidiaries) who have won the Malcolm Baldrige National Quality Award since 1988, the 14 publicly traded companies clearly outperformed the S&P 500 companies by greater than four to one. The five whole companies performed even better, outperforming the S&P 500 by more than five to one (National Institute of Standards 1996).

National Quality Award as a framework for improving higher education (Seymour 1996), and implementing the quality principles has made a significant and positive difference for these institutions.

TABLE 1

Higher Education Institutions among the First to Adopt the Quality Principles

Alabama State University	Marietta College
Arkansas State University	Northwest Missouri State University
Arkansas Tech University	Oregon State University
Babson College	The Pennsylvania State University
Belmont University	St. John Fisher College
Brazosport College	Samford University
Central Connecticut State University	Southern College of Technology
Clemson University	United States Air Force Academy
Colorado State University	University of Chicago
Cornell University	University of Illinois-Chicago
Dallas County Community College District	University of Maryland
Delaware County Community College	University of Michigan
Duke University	University of Minnesota-Duluth
El Camino Community College	University of Minnesota-Twin Cities
Fordham University	University of Montevallo
Fox Valley Technical College	University of Pennsylvania
George Mason University	University of Tampa
Georgia Institute of Technology	University of Wisconsin-Madison
Grand Rapids Junior College	University of Wyoming
Lamar Community College	Winona State University
Maricopa County Community College District	

Organization of This Report

The quality movement has been given a variety of labels, among them "total quality management" (TQM), "continuous quality improvement," (CQI), and, in this monograph, "the quality principles." This report describes, through an extensive review of the literature and by incorporating the results of a national survey, how institutions can create a culture for academic excellence by implementing the quality principles in higher education. The first section, "The History of the Quality Movement," explains the historical significance of the quality movement in relationship to business and industry. "What Is Quality?" defines quality as it relates to higher education institutions, and "The Evolution of Quality in Higher Education" describes how the quality movement has evolved among postsecondary institutions. "Creating a

Quality Culture" identifies the components of an institutional culture, describes how to build a culture that supports the quality principles, and briefly explains each principle. "The Shifting Paradigm" discusses the change in thinking that is a prerequisite to initiating the quality approach on campus. The following eight sections explain each of the eight quality principles in the context of higher education. The underlying premise is that the principles, used as a total system, form the foundation of quality improvement. The final section, "Implications of Implementing the Quality Principles," integrates the lessons learned from practitioners committed to the quality principles, enabling readers to benefit from the practical experiences of administrators and faculty engaged in and dedicated to implementing the quality principles in higher education.

THE HISTORY OF THE QUALITY MOVEMENT

Quality is not just an output, but a mind-set and work process that ensures the speed and flexibility consumers now expect. Organizations must run faster to deliver what the customer wants, but must also run longer, because the competition keeps moving the "finish line" farther away—"a race without a finish line" (Schmidt and Finnigan 1992, pp. xii–xiii).

The quality principles individually are not new, but in combination they are a new philosophical way of thinking about how organizations operate—an example of a whole greater than the sum of its parts. In business and industry, the quality movement is a new paradigm of management. W. Edwards Deming referred to it as "the third Industrial Revolution" (Schmidt and Finnigan 1992). Quality products have always been prized, but the philosophy of quality is primarily a post–World War II phenomenon.

After World War II, American business and industry held a competitive advantage over other countries, the market seemed almost limitless, and the quality of products did not seem so important when customers were waiting to be able to buy them. It was easy to succeed in this business environment; in fact, it was almost impossible to fail. The United States had the largest market, superior technology, more highly skilled workers, more wealth, and the best managers of the industrialized countries (Dertouzos, Lester, and Solow 1989).

At the same time, Japan was intent on improving its economy through manufacturing and trade; however, Japanese products were inferior to what was being produced in the West. Through the Japanese Federation of Economic Organizations and the Union of Japanese Scientists and Engineers, Japanese companies acted together to send teams to visit foreign companies to study their approaches to managing for quality, translate foreign literature into Japanese, and invite foreign lecturers, such as W. Edwards Deming and Joseph M. Juran, to Japan to conduct training courses on such topics as statistics and managing for quality (Juran 1995a). Deming and Juran influenced Japanese management and, in turn, were influenced by Japanese quality experts and by Japanese management concepts.

The Japanese readily embraced the theories of Deming and Juran as well as input from their own experts on quality. The quality culture that resulted propelled Japan into a position of leadership in the world marketplace by the late 1970s. Management theories and practices that once seemed idealistic and academic were shown to work extremely well.

How did Japanese companies progress so quickly? The Japanese adopted six strategies that led to the revolution (Juran 1995a):

1. Upper managers took charge of leading the revolution.
2. Companies trained their engineers and workers in statistical methods for quality control (Deming's 1950 lectures were the seed courses).
3. Entire managerial hierarchies were trained in how to manage for quality (Juran's 1954 lectures were the seed courses).
4. Quality improvement was undertaken at a revolutionary rate, year after year.
5. The workforce was allowed to participate in quality improvement through quality control circles (a contribution of Japanese quality expert Kaoru Ishikawa).
6. Companies included quality goals in their business plans.

Some have said that if Deming and Juran had not given their lectures in Japan, the Japanese quality revolution would not have occurred. But Juran himself disagrees:

> *Had the Americans never gone there, the Japanese quality revolution would have taken place without them. Each of the Americans did bring to Japan a structured training package that the Japanese had not yet evolved. In that sense, each gave the Japanese a degree of jump-start. But the same Americans also gave their lectures in other countries, none of which succeeded in building such a revolution. . . . The unsung heroes of the Japanese quality revolution are the Japanese managers* (Juran 1995a, p. 36).

It was those managers who put all the ideas together into a quality culture.

In the late 1970s and 1980s, many American companies began to understand that they could not survive unless they changed their ways of doing business. The principles of quality management that were originally formulated in the United States were brought back to this country and applied in many companies. The momentum of the quality movement in the United States was fueled by the competitive and global marketplace in which American projects were falling behind higher-quality products, primarily made in Japan. These products were less costly to manufacture, sold at lower prices, and produced much faster than American products. People in the United States began to prefer the foreign products, not only because they were cheaper, but also because they were better. The demand for American products fell, and American manufacturers found themselves in the unfamiliar role of playing catch-up with foreign manufacturers. To add to their difficulty, customers started to demand even higher levels of quality as their expectations continued to rise (Schmidt and Finnigan 1992).

American businesses turned to quality consultants—the three best known of which were Deming, Juran, and Philip Crosby—to help them save their companies. Each consultant contributed to the overall development of the quality movement. Deming's philosophy is based on an all-embracing concept of quality and an understanding of variation, combined in an environment in which teamwork, rather than competition, prevails (Deming 1986; Neave 1990; Walton 1986). His message to management was very simple: If you improve the quality of your goods and services, you will increase your productivity because there will be less scrap and less rework (see figure 1).

Juran's trilogy of quality planning, quality control, and quality improvement is the basis for his ideas on quality management. His philosophy stresses that employees must be involved in project teams, that managers must listen to employees and help them rank processes and systems that require improvement, and that managers must provide recognition to the entire task force after a project is completed (Juran 1988, 1989, 1992). Crosby popularized the idea that zero defects is the only acceptable performance standard, arguing that companies must do the right thing the first time and not depend upon inspection to find problems so they can be fixed (Crosby 1979, 1992).

Today, some American companies are world leaders because they have implemented quality principles, among them Federal Express, Hewlett-Packard, Intel, Milliken, Motorola, Saturn, and Xerox (Schmidt and Finnigan 1992).*

The quality principles are the integration of a number of management theories. Eleven management theories and practices have been identified as contributing to quality principles:

1. *Scientific management:* Finding the best way to do a job.
2. *Group dynamics:* Enlisting and organizing the power of group experience.
3. *Training and development:* Investing in human capital.
4. *Motivation through achievement:* Knowing that people attain satisfaction from accomplishment.
5. *Employees' involvement:* Giving workers some influence in the organization.
6. *Sociotechnical systems:* Operating organizations as open systems.
7. *Organizational development:* Helping organizations to learn and change.
8. *Corporate culture:* Knowing the beliefs, myths, and values that guide the behavior of people throughout the organization.
9. *The new leadership theory:* Inspiring and empowering others to act.
10. *The linking-pin concept of organization:* Creating cross-functional teams.
11. *Strategic planning:* Matching external challenges with internal strengths (Schmidt and Finnigan 1992).

These management theories and practices are part of the culture of organizations that are committed to the quality movement, including those that have won the Malcolm Baldrige National Quality Award (table 2).

*For more information on the history of the quality movement in business and industry, see Cornesky et al. 1991; Dobyns and Crawford-Mason 1991; Garvin 1988; Gitlow, Oppenheim, and Oppenheim 1995; Ishikawa 1985; Juran 1995b; Schmidt and Finnigan 1992; Wadsworth, Stephens, and Godfrey 1986.

FIGURE 1

The Deming Chain Reaction

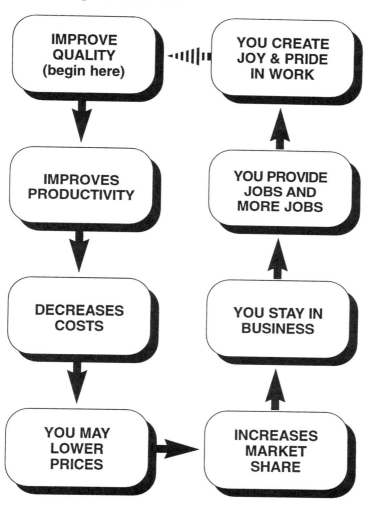

Source: Boardman 1994.

TABLE 2

Winners of the Malcolm Baldrige National Quality Award

Year	Category	Winner
1988	Manufacturing Manufacturing Small business	Motorola, Inc. Westinghouse Electric Corp. - Commercial Nuclear Fuel Division Globe Metallurgical, Inc.
1989	Manufacturing Manufacturing	Miliken & Co. Xerox Corp. - Business Products and Systems
1990	Manufacturing Manufacturing Service company Small business	General Motors - Cadillac Division IBM Rochester Federal Express Corp. Wallace Co.
1991	Manufacturing Manufacturing Small business	Solectron Corp. Zytec Corp. Marlow Industries
1992	Manufacturing Manufacturing Service company Service company Small business	AT&T Transmission Systems Business Unit Texas Instruments' Defense Systems and Electronics Group AT&T Universal Card Services Ritz-Carlton Hotel Granite Rock Co.
1993	Manufacturing Small business	Eastman Chemical Ames Rubber
1994	Service company Service company Small business	AT&T Consumer Communication Services GTE Directories Wainwright Industries
1995	Manufacturing Manufacturing	Armstrong Wold Industries' Building Production Operation Corning Telecommunications Products Division

WHAT IS QUALITY?

What is quality? People are willing to pay for it, organizations are driven to invest in it, workers are exhorted to produce it, and advertisers feel compelled to communicate it. Everyone wants it, but what is it? (Seymour 1993b, p. 6).

All this sounds like the Golden Rule to me (Carothers and Sevigny 1993, p. 15).

Definitions of Quality

Definitions of quality in the literature vary. It is:

- ". . . a predictable degree of uniformity and dependability at a low cost, suited to the market" (Deming 1986). How well do graduates meet the needs of their first employers?
- ". . . fitness for use, as judged by the user" (Juran 1989). Are the books in the bookstore before classes start?
- ". . . conformance to requirements" (Crosby 1979). Are all graduates able to pass examinations for certification into professional programs?
- ". . . full customer satisfaction" (Feigenbaum 1956). Are faculty needs for support services being met by the administration?
- ". . . continuing improvement involving everyone" (Imai 1986). Are members working together to improve processes and systems?
- ". . . a thought revolution in management" (Ishikawa 1985). Have institutions focused on value-added instead of input measures for success?

Within business and industry, quality is often thought of as best in class, how well an organization achieves its mission, exceeding stakeholders' expectations, continuous improvement, and a process, not just an outcome. Although they are each an important part of defining quality, these descriptions are insufficient in and of themselves.

Quality is defined by stakeholders (Deming 1986). Therefore, in continuous improvement, quality is a moving target because customers' perceptions continue to change and evolve. Fundamental to the quality principles is the inclusion of stakeholders' input "to engage in a continuous process that involves (1) determining how well needs and expectations are being met and (2) identifying where improvements are needed" (Ruben 1995a, p. 158).

If members of the academy view efforts to achieve quality as a cookie-cutter approach, the efforts will likely not succeed. The power of the quality principles is that they are based on stakeholders' expectations. When it becomes part of an organization's culture to have its vision, mission, and outcomes driven by stakeholders, the changing needs and expectations of stakeholders are automatically taken into consideration and changes are made accordingly. Quality is then seen as conceptually and pragmatically dependent upon meeting and exceeding stakeholders' expectations and requirements rather than the more arbitrary comparison to the competition (Ruben 1995a).

Quality is something people do (a verb) rather than a state of being (a noun) (Chaffee and Sherr 1992). "If an organization stops working to achieve quality, it begins to move away from having quality" (p. xx). Quality therefore is a concept of a state of being, an orientation and a philosophy focused on action.

Quality is a nebulous word like "excellent" or "outstanding," all of which are difficult to define. Yet it is important to define quality, because if it cannot be defined, then it cannot be measured. If quality cannot be measured, it cannot be achieved. And if quality cannot be achieved, the cost of poor quality continues to erode future opportunities for an institution (Berry 1991). An organization that can define, measure, and achieve quality in conjunction with monitoring stakeholders' perceptions will earn and sustain a strong competitive advantage. Two kinds of quality exist—quality in fact and quality in perception—and it is not possible to have total quality unless both are present (Reynolds 1992).

Higher education institutions use four criteria to define quality (Bergquist 1995). The oldest measurement concerns the *input* of resources—for example, grade point averages or standardized test scores of entering students, terminal degrees of faculty, number of books in the library, or size of the institution's endowment—into an institution. *Outputs* are the second traditional measurement of quality; they include such items as the overall graduation rate, the number of graduates going on to "the best" graduate schools, the number of faculty publications or research grants, the number of scholarly awards, or the number of graduates leading *For-tune* 500 companies.

More recently, institutions have begun to measure quality by *value-added criteria* defined, not by some national standard, but through a comparison of the state of affairs before and after a process—for example, the intellectual development of a student from freshman year to graduation or an increased number of citizens employed as a result of the faculty's public service projects. Finally, some institutions are beginning to base the state of their quality on improvements in and effectiveness of their *processes* involving both academic and nonacademic portions of the institution. Thus, the quality of teaching would be measured, not by final grades, but by students' involvement, or the quality of the student aid office would be measured, not by total awards handled, but by how timely each award was administered.

Combining these four criteria results in the following definition of quality:

> *Quality exists in a college or university to the extent that adequate and appropriate resources are being directed successfully toward the accomplishment of mission-related institutional outcomes and that programs in the college or university make a significant and positive mission-related difference in the lives of people affiliated with the college or university and are created, conducted, and modified in a manner that is consistent with the mission (and values) of the institution* (Bergquist 1995, p. 44).

The value of Bergquist's definition of quality is that it not only develops a relationship among the four criteria most often used to measure quality, but also sees quality as an ongoing process. The definition falls short, however, because it does not define quality as an integral part of an organization's culture.

Summary
The quality principles provide a comprehensive way to develop an understanding of quality as both a personal philosophy and a culture change. Continuous improvement and, more specifically, total quality management are being used

More recently, institutions have begun to measure quality by value-added criteria defined . . . through a comparison of the state of affairs before and after a process . . .

as quick fixes instead of focusing on needed long-term changes in the culture to improve quality. The focus of this monograph is on an examination of the quality principles as the underlying foundation of the quality movement. The principles are simple, not new, and based on common sense. The real challenge is to create a quality culture that incorporates *all* the principles and applies them in a disciplined manner.

THE EVOLUTION OF QUALITY IN HIGHER EDUCATION

The financial health of virtually every American college or university depends directly on tuition-paying, appropriation-generating undergraduate students. Giving undergraduates good value for what they, their parents, and the public invest in higher education is the single most important thing the institution can do to get out of "the mess" (Leslie and Fretwell 1996, p. 26).

Similar to the implementation of long-range planning in the late 1970s and strategic planning in the mid-1980s, higher education is influenced by the experiences of business and industry in their use of the quality principles. Stiff competition through the introduction of better products from foreign countries gave American businesses the impetus to become involved in quality; competition for students from other institutions of higher education and the desire to enhance the institution has given American colleges and universities the impetus to investigate the quality principles. Many institutions that are in the forefront of implementing the quality principles were encouraged by business leaders. In some instances, institutions were criticized because their graduates were not educated in the quality principles. In other cases, institutions were asked to help teach the quality principles to employees in certain companies. In still other situations, businesses encouraged colleges and universities to try implementing the quality principles as a more effective way of operating the institution.

At the end of the 1980s and the beginning of the 1990s, the quality movement in higher education existed only on the fringes of campus concerns. In most institutions where an awareness of quality principles existed, the awareness came from outside sources, such as books and articles on quality. Few institutions were involved in practicing the principles. But interest in the quality movement exploded in 1991 and 1992, as evidenced by the results of a national survey on TQM on campus (Freed, Klugman, and Fife 1994). In this survey of over 400 institutions that were identified as having shown interest in the quality principles, 25 percent of the responding institutions reported that they began implementation of the principles in 1990 or before 1990, 50 percent reported that they began in 1991 or 1992, and 25 percent reported that they began in 1993 and early 1994. During the late 1980s and early 1990s, institutions questioned whether the quality movement was appropriate for education. Just a few years later, administrators asked not whether the quality movement was appropriate, but *how* to make the quality principles relevant and worthwhile to their campuses (American Association 1994). As the momentum continued to grow, institutions with individual success stories were able to stimulate interest in other institutions (American Association 1994).

The first three institutions to become thoroughly involved in the quality movement seemingly were Northwest Missouri State University in 1984, Fox Valley Technical College in 1986, and Oregon State University in 1989. Although these three institutions differ in size, location, and type of degrees offered, they all had presidents who developed an interest in the quality movement, became champions of quality within their own institutions, and applied the quality principles with a long-term commitment (Hubbard 1993).

The early followers on the quality journey were a mix of community colleges, four-year private colleges and universities, and four-year public schools. Although distinctively different, each institution found the quality principles appropriate to its situation. A number of the institutions have been surveyed and have provided in-depth information about why they became interested in the quality movement (American Association 1994; Seymour 1993b; Seymour and Collett 1991). Table 1 (p. 15) provides a list of institutions that participated in these studies.

A wide variety of external influences led institutions to embrace the quality movement (Hoffman and Julius 1995). Criticism, encouragement, and pressure from businesses were often cited as reasons in institutions located in metropolitan areas. Public institutions cited legislative and public demands for accountability because of the significant state funds being allocated to public institutions. These same institutions cited reduced support from state governments as an additional impetus to implement the quality principles. Along the same lines, some schools faced declining enrollments because of increased competition and a declining population base. And other schools cited reaccreditation and advice from college advisory boards (American Association 1994; Freed, Klugman, and Fife 1994; Seymour and Collett 1991).

Internal influences that led institutions to embrace the quality principles were also quite varied. Several institutions recognized the irony that they taught quality improvement but did not practice what they taught. Many realized that they needed to improve processes within their institutions, others sought to improve services for stakeholders, and still others sought to achieve the institution's vision and mission. Many institutions wanted to eliminate the duplication of effort in academic and administrative areas and thereby increase the organization's efficiency (American Association 1994; Freed, Klugman, and Fife 1994; Seymour and Collett 1991).

Interest in implementing the quality principles continues to evolve, as seen in the annual Quality in Education Survey by *Quality Progress.* Since 1991, *Quality Progress* has conducted a survey to determine how many community colleges and four-year public and private colleges and universities offer courses in quality improvement and whether they apply the quality principles in managing their institutions. The number of participants has steadily increased over the five years: community colleges from 14 to 83 and four-year colleges and universities from 78 to 220. Eighty-eight percent of the four-year colleges and universities that responded in 1995 reported using the quality principles to manage their administrations, 55 percent offer quality-related certificates, minors, or degrees, and 42 percent do both. Among community colleges, 91 percent of respondents use quality principles to manage their administrations, 66 percent offer quality-related certificates, minors, or degrees, and 52 percent do both (Calek 1995).

In response to this increased interest in the quality movement during 1990 to 1992, the American Association for Higher Education (AAHE) and the William C. Norris Institute collaborated to create the Academic Quality Consortium (AQC) in January 1993. The purpose of AQC is to provide campuses committed to implementing quality in higher education with the opportunity to exchange information, build on one another's experiences, expand on assessment practices already used, and share the results of their work with the wider higher education community. Seventeen institutions were part of AQC when it began in 1993; in fall 1996 there were 20 members (see table 3). These institutions have gained experience in pursuing quality and provide a learning laboratory for sharing among the most advanced practitioners. Initial work focused on establishing an annual national conference on continuous quality improvement and the assessment of learning each June. The 11th Annual

AAHE Conference on Assessment and Quality was held in 1996; it was the fourth annual conference incorporating quality as well as assessment.

TABLE 3

Current Members of the Academic Quality Consortium

Alverno College	Northwest Missouri State University
Babson College	Oregon State University
Belmont University	Pennsylvania State University
Clemson University	Rutgers University
Dallas County Community College District	St. John Fisher College
Delaware County Community College	Samford University
Georgia Institute of Technology	University of Michigan
Maricopa County Community Colleges	University of Minnesota-Twin Cities
Marietta College	University of Wisconsin-Madison
Miami University	Winona State University

A primary way this group shares its experiences and knowledge of quality practices is through the AAHE Continuous Quality Improvement (CQI) Project. An e-mail discussion list open to all educators interested in quality improvement in higher education, CQI-L, was started in January 1994. The group began with a membership of approximately 50 and had grown to approximately 750 members in fall 1996. In January 1995, the CQI Project announced the formation of the Campus Quality Coordinators Network (CoordNet). CoordNet is open to only one person per campus; it was formed to provide campus quality coordinators with access to colleagues, information, new ideas, and assistance with the challenges of improving quality on their campuses. Within four weeks of its initiation, CoordNet had 55 members; as of fall 1996, it had 111 members. A second e-mail discussion list, Coord-L, was started in February 1995 for members of CoordNet. It is apparent from the growth of these groups that the interest in quality improvement in higher education continues to expand.

A number of community and technical colleges that were in the process of implementing quality improvement formed the Continuous Quality Improvement Network of Community and Technical Colleges (CQIN) in 1990. The purposes of CQIN are to assist member CEOs with active organizational transformation through outside-the-box learning and the sharing of best practices, and to enhance active institutional learning for faculty, staff, and trustees. The organization meets twice each year, once for a summer institute that discusses a learning theme and a second time (for the CEOs) that addresses issues of leadership and a particular subject related to learning organizations and continuous quality improvement. As of fall 1996, 26 institutions and two community college districts were members of CQIN.

Another organization that seeks to promote quality in higher education is the National Association of College and University Business Officers (NACUBO). Through its offerings of professional development workshops for administrators and its annual meeting, NACUBO stresses process improvement and highlights innovative ideas that assist colleges and universities in offering new or better services to their students. The focus of the 1996 NACUBO annual meeting was on collaboration between colleges and universities and private industry, local businesses, government, and other organizations. In addition, NACUBO recognizes successful efforts to improve colleges and universities by each year awarding quality improvement of departmental and campus programs; process improvement through reengineering, redesign, and restructuring; and cost reduction, enhanced revenue, and improved productivity initiatives. NACUBO's Benchmarking project provides institutions with an opportunity to compare themselves with other institutions as well as to measure their improvement over time. NACUBO's full membership is approximately 2,660 organizations, with 2,100 of them colleges and universities.

Closely allied with quality in higher education is assessment, and "an assessment plan is a means to the end of continuous improvement" (Lovett 1994, p. 6). Although the assessment movement in higher education took hold much earlier than the quality movement, its objectives are an integral part of the quality principles. Whereas the assessment movement has concentrated on the academic side, focusing on improving teaching and learning, the quality principles include continuous assessment of both the academic and the nonacademic side of the academy. Because the quality techniques were perceived to be management tools, the quality principles were first applied in administration and only later in the academic areas (Seymour 1991; Seymour and Collett 1991). Sixty-eight percent of responding institutions in one survey had used the quality principles in at least one area within both administrative and academic parts of the organization, 10 percent in academic areas only, and 22 percent in administrative areas only (Freed, Klugman, and Fife 1994). Furthermore, 38 percent of the institutions reported that the quality principles had been used by at least one faculty member in classroom instruction.

The beginning of the assessment movement in higher education is associated with the publication of two national reports, *Involvement in Learning* (National Institute of Education 1984) and *Integrity in the College Curriculum* (Association of American Colleges 1985). These reports called for major changes in the contents and coherence of curricula. They also called for a new look at the breadth of knowledge, skills, and attitudes that all graduates should possess in common (Ewell 1991).

External pressure for assessment came from business and industry in complaints about the decline in the quality of graduates. Government became involved in 1986 with the publication of reports by the Education Commission of the States and the National Governors Association promoting assessment as a means to make institutions accountable to the public.

In response to these internal and external pressures on higher education, many institutions developed assessment programs. One consequence of the external pressure on institutions to create plans to assess students' learning was that institutions developed negative attitudes toward assessment and adopted bureaucratic approaches to it (Lovett 1994). To save time, institutions began with programs that used standardized tests. It was only after seeing the limitations of end-point testing that they began to try alternatives that included measures of input and behavior (Ewell 1991).

Just as the implementation of the quality principles in higher education moved from the adoption of techniques directly from business and industry to a systemic approach to quality improvement, assessment moved from entirely outcome-based programs to more informative process-based programs. A process-based assessment approach involves three steps (Ewell 1991). First is the increased reliance on systematic process indicators to make sense of outcomes—which does not mean that outcomes are abandoned but that measurements are first taken to assess the standards at the beginning of a process (baseline measurements) and are followed up with additional measures to monitor how well the process is working. Second is the increasing reliance on natural settings for gathering information, which includes using the network of existing points of contact with students to gather data on students and periodically to collect examples of students' actual work in portfolios. Third is the increased use of classroom assessment to improve teaching and learning through frequent checks of how well students are meeting the goals of instruction (Cross 1994). Individual instructors can periodically collect information from their students, using many methods of feedback (Angelo and Cross 1993). The strengths of classroom assessment techniques, which are fundamental to the quality principles, are that individual faculty members have more control over the results. Because faculty manage the classroom process themselves, ongoing process information—the results of which the faculty member can quickly respond to—is less threatening than information about outcomes, which comes too late for any faculty intervention.

Classroom and institutional assessment and the tools and techniques of the quality movement provide data that can enable an institution to improve. These two approaches work together within the framework of interrelated and continuous academic quality management (Dill 1992) (see figure 2). Traditional educational systems are linear. In this system, students are educated through a program that features specific educational processes. The students are then placed in jobs with employers, who are major customers of and stakeholders in the success of this educational process. Under the traditional, linear approach, employers usually have little input into the content of the curriculum and therefore become major critics of the process.

In an academic quality management model or system, employers are seen as important assessors of the results of the education process and therefore are included in the process. As a consequence, educational programs are continuously designed and redesigned based on a combination of stakeholders' expectations and faculty knowledge and expertise. Institutional assessment produces measures of students' performance at various points in the educational program when changes can still be made that will improve the results for individual students. As such, assessment provides data for improving students' learning. The tools and techniques of quality are used in the study of particular educational processes that contribute to the overall educational program. The quality principles guide the management of the entire system, from students to stakeholders (Dill 1992).

FIGURE 2

Stages of Contemporary Quality Management in Higher Education

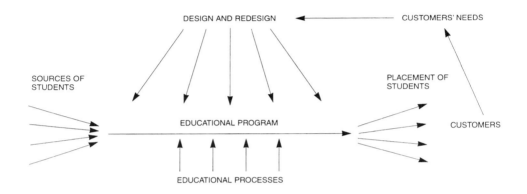

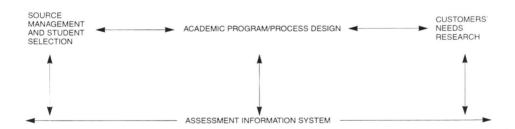

Source: Dill 1992 (adapted from Deming 1986).

*Exemplary presidents give equal attention to task and
relationships, and [they] have a collaborative relationship with the faculty. Their continued willingness to
listen and be influenced serves as a source of renewal
of their moral authority and interpretive capabilities*
(Birnbaum 1992, p. 159).

Culture is "the cumulative perception of how the organization treats people and how people expect to treat one another. It is based on consistent and persistent management
action, as seen by employees, vendors, and customers"
(Sashkin and Kiser 1993, p. 111). Culture is the collective
programming of the mind (Hodgetts 1993); this collective
programming is an inferential concept that is perceived and
felt, often invisible but binding. "Culture is usually defined
as social or normative glue that holds an organization together" (Smircich 1983, p. 344). The culture is based on values and beliefs that members share. Institutional culture is
the set of goals and values to which, ideally, all employees
are committed. It need not be set down as written principles
or guidelines, but it must be anchored in the heads (cogni-
tively) and the hearts (emotionally) of all employees and
respected by leaders and followers alike (Simon 1996).

A lack of understanding about the role of organizational
culture in improving management and institutional performance inhibits the ability to address the challenges facing
higher education. Because an institution's culture is reflected
in what is done, how it is done, and who is involved in doing it, culture plays a central role in the quality improvement
movement (Atkinson 1990; Crouch 1992, p. 29). When they
understand the connection between culture and continuous
improvement, leaders are better able to make decisions consistent with the values of the existing culture while working
to create a new culture (Chaffee and Tierney 1988).

A cultural shift is taking place. Organizations are moving
from a focus on product to a focus on market, which has
required managers to shift from managing to leading and
from directing employees to empowering them (Steeples
1992). In higher education, culture has been referred to as
the "invisible tapestry" that weaves together all parts and
members of the institution (Kuh and Whitt 1988). More
specifically, culture in higher education is:

. . . the collective, mutually shaping patterns of norms, values, practices, beliefs, and assumptions that guide the behavior of individuals and groups in an institute of higher education and provide a frame of reference within which to interpret the meaning of events and actions on and off campus (Kuh and Whitt 1988, pp. 12–13).

Institutional culture is the fabric that weaves and supports the quality principles into institutional practices and behaviors.

The culture of a college or university is its chosen paradigm, those perspective patterns or interpretative constructs [that] provide a matrix of meaning for shared activities. . . . This is why the highest task of leadership is to shape a robust culture congruent with the mission of the institution (Hull 1995, p. 3).

All the foregoing definitions of culture emphasize that organizations develop distinctive beliefs and patterns over time. Many of the patterns and assumptions act as an "unconscious infrastructure" (Kuh and Whitt 1988) and are often taken for granted. They are reflected in myths, tales, stories, rituals, or ceremonies. The major components of organizational culture emerge through the vision and principles of the leaders (Argyris 1976; Bennis 1983; Davis 1984; Schein 1983). Leaders need to understand the significance of the institutional culture because it affects how members think, feel, and act. The culture serves as an organizing framework for determining rewards and punishments, what is valued and what is not, and moral guidelines that bond individuals and groups and influence behaviors (Kuh and Whitt 1988).

Because a strong culture is powerful in guiding behavior, it helps employees perform at a higher level in two ways. First, a strong culture is a system of informal rules that specifies how people are to behave most of the time. Therefore, employees waste little time deciding how to act, and they are more productive. Second, people can feel better about what they do, so they are more likely to work harder. The strong standards and related value system provide a productive environment in which to work (Deal and Kennedy 1982).

A Culture of Shared Values

A quality culture needs leaders who involve and empower employees in continually improving processes. Leaders create a community where members want to enroll in the shared institutional vision. They understand that employees' satisfaction is a prerequisite to customers' satisfaction (Reynolds 1992). A strong sense of disciplinary communication, the hallmark of academic institutions, is being replaced by a sense of campus community. Institutions are building this community through identifying common interests and sharing experiences.

A recent study examining two types of colleges exemplifies the power of creating a culture based on shared mission and core values. In the first type of college, faculty morale was low even though salaries were high, teaching loads were moderate, and resources were abundant; in the second, faculty morale was high although salaries were low, teaching loads were overwhelming, and resources were scarce. The distinguishing factor between the two types of institutions was that the one with higher morale had a shared mission and a widely shared set of core values (Deal and Jenkins 1994).

Leaders create a community where members want to enroll in the shared institutional vision.

A Culture without Fear

Effective organizations require open and honest communication (McGregor 1967), communication that depends on "a climate of mutual trust and support with the group . . . [where] members can be themselves without fearing the consequences" (p. 192). Trust is the prime catalyst for increasing productivity and quality in any organization (Graham and LeBaron 1994). Deming, in his 14 principles, asserts that quality is impossible when people are afraid to tell the truth, when fear permeates the workplace. Fear arises from a situation in which people "feel threatened by possible repercussions [if they speak] up about work-related concerns" (Ryan and Oestreich 1991, p. 21). The quality of the relationship between an employee and his or her supervisor is often directly related to the fear or lack of fear that a person experiences at work.

The traditional hierarchical system enabled "the boss" to set the tone of the culture, and over time employees became culturally programmed not to trust their bosses. "Our national culture dictates an active mistrust of hierarchy and conformity and an appreciation of competition and rebellion" (Ryan and Oestreich 1991, p. 35). In the relationship between boss and subordinate, a win-lose mentality encourages complaints and blame rather than cooperation and trust. A them-versus-us attitude does not lead to collaborative problem solving.

Even entry-level people have a perception and concern about what leaders at the top of the organization are doing (Ryan and Oestreich 1991). Members perceive top management as having little effect on daily activities, but their perceptions influence how they think they will be treated daily. If members of the organization do not trust upper management, they will have an underlying fear that in turn affects outcomes. "If the behaviors employees see from managers are abrasive, abusive, or ambiguous, the patterns of fear become more entrenched" (p. 84), resulting in patterns that are difficult to break.

A Culture of Inclusiveness

Some organizations looking for a quick fix mistakenly focus on changing quality-related behaviors—changing the reporting structure or some work processes, for example—rather than changing underlying values, beliefs, and assumptions about continuous quality improvement. Changing a culture involves changing the patterns of norms, values, practices, beliefs, and assumptions that guide behaviors.

> *Behavioral changes involve changing behavior without making the corresponding changes in the underlying values, beliefs, and assumptions that make up the culture. While there are situations when behavioral change is sufficient in the short term, it is difficult and expensive to maintain in the long run. This is because the values and beliefs remain the same, and managers must spend significant amounts of time and energy on monitoring and controlling behavior* (Neal and Tromley 1995, p. 45).

In a culture of continuous improvement, administrators shift from controlling behaviors to empowering and including others. Members engage in self-management because they understand their role in the overall institutional system.

A five-year study of presidential leadership in 32 colleges and universities found that one of the chief reasons for unsuccessful leadership was incongruence between the leader and the institutional culture (Birnbaum 1992). While the main reason for the failure of presidencies was taking decisive action without consulting with key stakeholders, usually early in a presidential career before a firm foundation of trust had been established, it was not true of successful presidents.

> *The most important characteristic of exemplary presidents is that they are seen as continuing to respond to the faculty and willing to open themselves to faculty influence. They listen to faculty, and they support existing faculty governance mechanisms. While modal [average] presidents are likely to treat communication and interaction as instrumental devices [that] become less important once they have learned about the campus, exemplary presidents are more likely to view them as essential and continuing components of evolving communities. The model president sees communication as a means to an end; the exemplary president sees it as an end to itself* (Birnbaum 1992, p. 98).

Exemplary presidents appreciated the importance of understanding the organization's culture, constantly communicating with that culture so the president could be better understood, and working within the culture to produce a shared vision.

Influencing the Culture

Because leaders construct and reinforce the culture by their daily actions, they need to be cognizant of how culture is constructed. Otherwise, they may send incorrect or misunderstood messages. Leaders unknowingly can create a workplace full of fear. Because actions often speak louder than words, leaders need to be aware of their actions, and they need to be careful that the appropriate message is being perceived. Therefore, culture is created by its leadership. Institutions can quickly communicate priorities, values, and assumptions by consistently linking rewards to desired behaviors (Schein 1985). People tend to demonstrate and repeat behaviors that are rewarded. Specifically:

- What leaders consider important, measure, and control sends messages to employees.
- How leaders react to institutional crises creates norms and values and reveals important underlying assumptions.
- How leaders act demonstrates their assumptions and values. Whether leaders are perceived as role models, teachers, or coaches depends on their behaviors.
- The criteria leaders establish for allocating rewards and status reinforce the culture (Schein 1985).

An institutional culture is a system based on perceived reality, not necessarily what is promoted, published, or preached. Leaders' clarity and consistency influence the culture. When changing the culture by changing the values and assumptions learned, leaders need to live the new values themselves. Institutions committed to the quality principles have leaders who understand the important role of creating a supportive culture. When presidents are committed to building a quality culture, their actions facilitate and encourage the empowerment and involvement of others. They can take certain actions to empower others:

- Using e-mail extensively to communicate with all constituents;
- Consistently surveying employees, students, and staff;
- Continually forming teams to solve issues and to make decisions;
- Constantly focusing on driving fear out of the organization;
- Committing resources (time and money) to systematic individual development so that employees will produce at their maximum capability (Freed, Klugman, and Fife 1995).

Changing an existing culture is a difficult and time-consuming task. "If the existing culture is incompatible with the intended changes, it can derail even the most well-planned efforts" (Neal and Tromley 1995, p. 45). To develop a culture that supports the quality principles, leaders must be perceptive and aware of the organization's dysfunctional elements. They must also have the emotional strength to deal with the anxiety associated with change and be willing to take the risks connected with change. Because leaders are likely targets of anger, they must stand strong and demonstrate their new assumptions for the institution.

Studies of efforts to change the organizational culture have found that while culture is not easily changed autocratically, culture is continually evolving as new members enter the institution with new beliefs, ideas, and assumptions (Kuh and Whitt 1988). Resistance to change can be reduced if employees understand how the changes will increase the effectiveness of the institution and ultimately be in their best interests—perhaps by leading to greater resources and more meaningful work. Unfortunately, in a competitive environment the focus is often on cutting costs and downsizing rather than on transforming the culture through developing employees' commitment and skills (Neal and Tromley 1995).

Creating a Culture of Excellence

In changing the culture of an institution, a long-term plan that describes behaviors in language that all participants understand is advantageous. Table 4 is an example of one organization's attempt to convert to a quality culture. The goal is to identify gaps between the current state and the future state to determine what needs to be changed to achieve the new culture. A plan to close the gaps is designed, and responsibilities are assigned. This course of action is consistent with what Deming (1986) refers to as "constancy of purpose"—a plan that clearly articulates the vision and describes the behaviors expected of members to achieve the vision and mission.

Recruitment and selection is one of the most important systems in building or changing a culture. In a quality culture, people are hired who are willing to learn and able to work in a team. New leaders are hired because their leadership style and philosophy fit the culture the organization is trying to create. Decisions about hiring are crucial for long-term cultural change. Selective recruitment of new faculty, administrators, and staff either maintains the cultural values or introduces different assumptions and beliefs to the institution, shaping the future development of the culture (Kuh and Whitt 1988; Neal and Tromley 1995).

Systematic development is an important element in creating and transforming a culture, because it provides members with knowledge, skills, and information needed to make the necessary changes. One frequently made mistake is to educate lower-level employees more than top leaders, resulting

TABLE 4

Vision for a New Culture

Category	Current state	Future state
Mission	Maximum return on investment/ management by objectives (ROI/MBO)	Ethical behavior and customer satisfaction; climate for continuous improvement; ROI a performance measure
Customer requirements	Incomplete or ambiguous understanding of customer requirements	Use of systematic approach to seek out, understand, and satisfy both internal and external customer requirements
Supplier objectives	Undirectional relationship Orientation to short-term objectives and actions with limited long-term perspective	Partnership Deliberate balance of long-term goals with successive short-term objectives
Improvement	Acceptance of process variability and subsequent corrective action assigning blame as the norm	Understanding and continually improving the process
Problem solving	Unstructured individualistic problem solving and decision making	Predominantly participative and interdisciplinary problem solving and decision making based on subsequent data
Jobs and people	Functional, narrow scope; management-controlled	Management and employee involvement; work teams; integrated functions
Management style	Management style with uncertain objectives, which instills fear of failure	Open style with clear and consistent objectives, which encourages group-derived continuous improvement
Role of the manager	Plan, organize, assign, control, and enforce	Communicate, consult, delegate, coach, mentor, remove barriers, and establish trust
Rewards and recognition	Pay by job; few team incentives	Individual and group recognition and rewards; negotiated criteria
Measurement	Orientation toward data gathering for problem identification	Data used to understand and continuously improve processes

Source: Schmidt and Finnigan 1992, p. 171.

in comparatively less understanding and commitment from the people who make the strategic decisions and control the resources. Often, members in the middle are also left out of the development effort. Another common mistake is to treat development as a one-time effort with little or no follow-up and reinforcement. In a quality culture, employees at all levels receive continual training and development to update their knowledge and skills; moreover, they are also involved in educating each other. Continuous learning is an important cultural norm in an environment that supports continuous quality improvement (Neal and Tromley 1995).

Because rewards influence behaviors, the reward system should be redesigned to encourage change in behaviors. This task is difficult in most organizations, but it is particularly difficult in higher education because of the long-standing traditions and practices. In a culture enforcing quality improvement, the system reinforces desired behaviors that contribute positively to a quality culture. The system is tied to the institution's mission, vision, and goals. Individuals are rewarded for working for the benefit of the entire system rather than for optimizing their area at the expense of the whole (Neal and Tromley 1995). The reward system plays an important role in creating a quality culture because people tend to behave according to how they are rewarded. For people to make the quality principles a priority, they must believe that the institution values and rewards these new behaviors. Even though changing the reward system is a complex task, the significance that rewards play in changing an institutional culture should be recognized.

Institutional culture provides stability for colleges and universities in turbulent times and contributes to the institution's general effectiveness by reminding students and faculty of what the institution values (Kuh and Whitt 1988). But changing the culture to support the quality movement is extremely difficult and time-consuming—a task that requires patience and determination. Cultural change, according to one college president, requires an intensive commitment from leaders. "Causing a cultural change, especially in a traditional institution, is a slow process, and not one for faint-hearted leadership" (Entner 1993, p. 34). Changing the culture usually produces conflict, because old cultures, habits, ideas, and practices rarely shift without some irritation. Nevertheless, this irritation should be perceived in a positive light, because it is a symptom of an organization that is changing, growing, and improving (Schmidt and Finnigan 1992).

Continuous improvement includes developing a mission that reflects stakeholders' expectations, making decisions based on data, viewing institutions as systems, and empowering people to take responsibility and to work in teams. Because effective communication is an essential element, all of the institution's communications, both in word and deed, must be consistent and must convey the notion that "this is a quality institution" (Schmidt and Finnigan 1992). A common mistake made by institutions in implementing the quality principles is to focus on just one or two principles—for example, data collection or teamwork or stakeholders' satisfaction—instead of implementing them holistically.

A quality culture exists when people know that they are fully and equally committed to each other's success. When they are, there is no room for fear to exist (Ryan and Oestreich 1991). Creating this kind of culture is the responsibility of leaders. Only when the senior leadership makes a real commitment to creating a quality culture by implementing all the quality principles as a total system will continuous improvement be attained and maintained (Sashkin and Kiser 1993).

The Quality Principles

Principles are guidelines for human conduct that are proven to have enduring, permanent value (Covey 1989, p. 35).

The power of continuous quality improvement, according to its proponents, lies in its principles—which fundamentally are a conceptual shift in how an organization is managed to achieve its vision, mission, and outcomes. *The quality principles are a personal philosophy and an organizational culture that use scientific measurement of outcomes, systematic management techniques, and collaboration to achieve the institution's mission.* Quality is a goal *and* a process. The goal is to continuously define, in measurable terms, the institution's and each of its subunit's missions, processes, and outcomes. Doing so is the act of living consciously. The process is implementing the quality principles: continuously measuring and improving the principles with a constant eye on the necessarily changing missions of the units and the institution. Doing so is the act of integrity: doing what we say we are doing.

The authorities most often mention the following eight principles (see, e.g., Chaffee and Sherr 1992; Cornesky et al.

1992; Crosby 1979; Deming 1986; Juran 1989; Seymour 1995). Organizations that subscribe to the quality principles:

- Are *vision, mission, and outcomes driven.* All organizations, especially social organizations like education institutions, exist for a purpose.* An organization's vision, mission, and outcomes are defined by the expectations of all the stakeholders. They must be sensitive to the values and culture of the organization and must ultimately be defined in measurable terms to provide for accountability. Without a clearly defined mission clarified by measurable outcomes, an organization lacks a clear sense of direction and focus.

  It is of utmost importance that the mission be defined by those who have a personal interest in the organization's success—the stakeholders who benefit from an organization's achieving its mission. Their expectations should be taken into consideration in developing the institution's vision and mission and in determining the outcomes of the systems and processes. For higher education institutions, stakeholders include faculty, students, administrators, staff, parents, trustees or regents, alumni, employers, funding agencies, and society in general. Each plays a significant role in helping ensure that the integrity of the institution is preserved by delivering what it promises. Because quality is based on the perception of those served by the institution, the expectations of stakeholders must be systematically monitored and analyzed when defining the institution's mission and outcomes.

- Are *systems dependent.* How well an institution performs is the result of how well its procedures and members interact as part of an interdependent system or process.† Because a change in one part of the institution affects the other parts, most problems in an organization are a result of problems with the work processes or systems, not with the people. For example, a problem with the system is

---

*Winners of the Malcolm Baldrige National Quality Award consistently state that the reason they believe in the quality principles is that the principles help keep them focused on why their businesses exist and not solely on the bottom line. Profit is important, but it is only a side outcome of a business's achieving its mission.

†The words "system" and "process" are used interchangeably to signify an interrelationship of two or more people working to achieve a common end. Within a process or system might also exist mutually exclusive processes or goals that must be resolved to achieve the common end.

apparent when faculty are rewarded for delivering papers at conferences but travel funds are frozen, or when students are expected to participate in team projects but have not developed the skills necessary for working in teams and are graded as individuals.

- Have *leaders who create a quality culture.* A different kind of leadership is needed to create a quality culture. Top-down leadership combined with bottom-up leadership is necessary for members to participate in making decisions and in improving processes and systems. Leaders must evaluate the current organizational culture with stakeholders' defined vision, mission, and outcomes in mind. To the extent the current culture is incongruent with the organization's purpose, the leader is responsible for systematically bringing the culture in harmony with that purpose. Leaders are responsible for helping the members understand that new ways of thinking and behaving are necessary to achieve the vision, mission, and outcomes.

- Exhibit *systematic individual development.* Because an organization is constantly changing, it is necessary to update continuously all its members' knowledge and skills to meet the demands of those changes and to prepare systematically for future changes. Doing so requires all members to be involved in individual development, such as education and training. If the organization does not provide education and training, individuals cannot perform effectively through no fault of their own. A lack of training should be perceived as a problem with the system.

- Make *decisions based on fact.* The real issues or basic causes of a problem cannot be identified or clearly understood unless all relevant data are gathered systematically. Three types of data are necessary before a problem can be understood rationally: (1) data measuring the desired outcomes; (2) data measuring the process; and (3) data that develop a contextual understanding. But it is a basic principle that data alone are meaningless. Data must be put into some context, have a proven relationship, and be seen as action and reaction before they have meaning. "Information, no matter how complete and speedy, is not knowledge. Knowledge has temporal spread. Knowledge comes from theory. Without theory, there is no way to use the information that comes to us on the instant" (Deming 1993, p. 109).

- *Delegate decision making.* If individuals are to be made responsible for achieving the mission, they must be made aware of how their position and actions relate to the mission and be given the flexibility to make the necessary changes to do their jobs. The more individuals sense they can influence a process, the more they take ownership for the successful conclusion of that process. But members need to gain the necessary knowledge and skills to be equipped to make informed decisions. Through continuous development, the parties responsible for a process understand better their areas of responsibility; the closer a person is to actual issues, the more knowledgeable that person is about the decisions needed to improve the process.
- *Collaborate.* Collaboration and teamwork produce results when individuals who have a stake in the outcome are involved in making decisions that influence the outcome. Teams divide labor, based on individual strengths, to achieve a common goal, whereas groups or committees share common information but not necessarily common goals. Collaboration is the result of those who have a vested interest in an objective working together to achieve mutually satisfying results. For example, the members of a collaborative team established to examine an institution's student financial aid program would include, at some point, the director and staff members of the financial aid office, students who have received aid and are applying for aid, staff of the admissions office, the institution's financial and budget staff, representatives of sources of financial aid, organizations that process applications for aid, and high school counselors. Including people who can directly and indirectly influence a process ensures a greater chance of their understanding all the facts about the process and, once a decision is made, have greater ownership for the success of that decision.
- *Plan for change.* A fundamental assumption of the quality principles is that an institution's mission is based on stakeholders' expectations. Because it is assumed that these expectations change constantly, it is logical to assume that an organization's mission also constantly evolves—sometimes slowly, sometimes rapidly. Institutions need to embrace change as a cultural value; they need to perceive change as positive and to anticipate it

daily. Planning for change is a fundamental assumption of continuous improvement.

- Have *leaders who support a quality culture*. As they create a culture that embraces change and continuous improvement, senior leaders need to support the implementation of the quality principles by ensuring that the systems are in place and the necessary resources available. They must be willing to consistently articulate the quality principles and reward their implementation. For most organizations, initial implementation of the quality principles translates into a fundamental change in the way business is conducted, and although it usually requires a change in culture, it might also require a change in support systems. For this change to occur and be sustained, top leaders must be constantly aware that they must consistently support those who are making the changes. One of the main priorities for top management should be to develop internal programs to teach the new philosophy to all employees (Aguayo 1990). The new leadership must be ready to reinforce, through rewards based on the quality principles, the changes necessary to make the quality principles a personal philosophy as well as an integral part of organizational values.

Thus, the quality principles can be visualized as a never-ending, continuous relationship:

The quality principles are systematically interrelated: New systems and processes lead to better quality. Better quality

increases pride and confidence, resulting in changed attitudes and behaviors. Behavioral changes positively influence the institution's culture. The changed and improved culture demands better systems and processes. This continuous cycle results in continuous improvement (Cornesky et al. 1992). Still, it is important to remember that the quality principles provide few answers. Rather, they involve asking different questions and providing potential methods for answering the questions (Chaffee and Sherr 1992).

THE SHIFTING PARADIGM

The significant problems we face cannot be solved at the same level of thinking we used when we created them.

—Albert Einstein

Definition of insanity: Doing the same thing, the same way, all the time—but expecting different results.

—Anonymous

If institutions are to implement the quality principles in both the administrative and academic areas, a new way of looking at and thinking about how higher education institutions function must occur. In other words, a paradigm shift is necessary. "Paradigm" comes from the Greek *paradeigma,* which means model, pattern, or example. A paradigm represents the way something is true; it is the mental map of its reality (Hodgetts, Luthans, and Lee 1994). For example, the world is flat, all watches must be regulated by tiny gears, and women are not intelligent enough to benefit from higher education are paradigms.

A paradigm establishes rules, defines boundaries, and describes how things behave within those boundaries (Barker 1992). An organizational paradigm involves the embodiment of shared ideas, values, and beliefs that are often referred to as its philosophy. The philosophy serves as a conceptual map that guides the behaviors of its members and drives the organization's structure and processes (Ketchum and Trist 1992).

Organizations where the paradigm has shifted to the quality principles have new rules, new boundaries, and new ways of behaving. As traditional organization charts flatten, work teams are developed across functional areas. These changes help everyone within the organization to understand work processes and their individual role in creating and improving quality—for example, when faculty move from a philosophy of passive learning to one of active learning. To gain students' involvement and therefore their greater ownership of the teaching/learning process, faculty must become more open about involving students and other faculty members in planning, executing, and evaluating courses.

"Mental models" is another analogy to explain a paradigm shift. Mental models are "deeply ingrained assumptions, generalizations, or even pictures or images that influence

An organizational paradigm involves the embodiment of shared ideas, values, and beliefs that are often referred to as its philosophy.

how we understand the world and how we take action" (Senge 1990, p. 8). To develop a new conceptualization, people must challenge their old ways of thinking or their assumptions (Russell and Evans 1992). If they are not analyzed, mental models or ways of thinking remain unchanged and the patterns continue. This concept is powerful because "structures of which we are unaware hold us prisoner" (Senge 1990, p. 60). When people recognize ineffective and/or inefficient patterns, the structures do not have the same hold on them and they can begin to alter behaviors to improve the situation. To shift the paradigm, people must experience a personal change.

Shifting the traditional paradigm or changing the mental model is central to understanding why people reject new ideas and resist change. Inevitably, a paradigm shift creates conflict and discomfort. And despite the positive results of a new paradigm, many members will cling to the old one (Ketchum and Trist 1992). When the quality principles are implemented, faculty and administrators must shift their thinking about the way work is done. Even though it takes time to break with the old, ingrained ideas, people begin to question their old assumptions and become open to new ways of thinking and acting (LeTarte 1993). Life under quality principles requires a shift from "If it ain't broken, don't fix it" to "Nothing stays perfect, so we must continuously work toward doing things better." A paradigm shift can be explained this way: "Suddenly I *saw* things differently, and because I *saw* differently, I *thought* differently, I *felt* differently, and I *behaved* differently" (Covey 1989, p. 31).

Changes have taken place in higher education in the past—for example, moving from studying the classics to a more modern curriculum including mathematics, chemistry, and engineering; allowing the use of calculators in mathematics and accounting classes; and teaching classes off the main campus. More recent examples include moving away from the traditional, passive lecture method to more active forms of cooperative learning; integrating various forms of technology, such as computers, in the classroom; introducing new curricula, such as women's studies, African-American studies, and environmental studies; moving from viewing education as a privilege to considering education a right; moving from perceiving students as products to perceiving them as stakeholders; changing from a rigid departmental structure to designing interdisciplinary courses; and moving from engaging in individual research to conducting collaborative scholarship.

These changes tend to evolve slowly and are often a challenge to implement because of the strong existing traditions or paradigms from the past. The shift to quality improvement is a challenge for similar reasons. Colleges and universities take pride in operating as a collection of isolated, individual parts. Even though autonomy and academic freedom are strengths at the foundation of the quality principles, these same characteristics, when exerted independently from the institution's overall mission, inhibit the organization's functioning effectively and responding quickly to stakeholders' changing expectations.

A major ingredient for change to occur is the presence of a "felt need." It is difficult to institute change where there is no perceived need for it. Research suggests that organizations do not change unless a clear, survival-based reason exists that involves organizational effectiveness (Lawler 1992; Nordvall 1982). Other obstacles stand in the way of implementing the quality principles in higher education: stakeholders with multiple—and sometimes conflicting—missions; faculty members' identification with academic areas and not with the institution's mission; and reward systems not related to accountability for a unit's mission.

For the quality principles to be effective, the culture and paradigm of higher education must change. In a quality culture, stakeholders' expectations must be continuously monitored. After stakeholders' expectations are known, a system must be developed to integrate their feedback into decision making. A quality culture encourages interdisciplinary efforts to support the mission. Then, incentives are developed to encourage faculty members to align their efforts with the institutional mission. Because rewards influence behaviors, reward systems are redesigned to reinforce members' efforts to accomplish objectives of the mission. For faculty, the historical debate about how to allocate time between teaching and research is clarified when institutions recognize improvements in teaching and reward them appropriately. From the perspective of quality, faculty development is a continuous process, and the tenure system in a quality culture allows innovation and encourages creativity by providing faculty the freedom to take risks and to make changes while holding them accountable for agreed-upon outcomes (Wolverton 1993).

The incentives for change in higher education are still too few, and implementation of the quality principles will continue to be slow until higher education "feels" a need to change (Ewell 1991). If they are going to be proactive in responding to environmental challenges, institutions must change their management practices—a change that involves new ways of conducting work, new standards, new systems, and new responsibilities. A quality culture encourages members to share ownership of the institution and to take responsibility for managing themselves, and faculty members and administrators must therefore be trained in the philosophy of continuous improvement. Learning new ways to measure outcomes to determine whether they are fulfilling their professional roles becomes part of the system. When it is translated into personal quality standards, quality becomes an internalized standard of excellence rather than a new management fad dictated from the top (Tice 1993).

The shifting paradigm is best illustrated by a story. A prospective student asked two professors in the English department what they taught. The first professor said, "I'm teaching Shakespeare." The second professor replied, "I'm teaching Shakespeare to help develop an appreciation of western civilization and critical thinking skills in my students, which will help them achieve a more successful life." In the new paradigm, the culture enables members to incorporate the institution's vision into their daily activities by understanding the significance of the institution's operation as a total system, with measurable outcomes, rather than isolated parts that operate independently.

VISION, MISSION, AND OUTCOMES DRIVEN

Nonprofit groups that give short shrift to their mission will almost always find the going bumpy. Those that invest the time and effort necessary to formulate a sound mission statement build a platform from which to soar (Knauft, Berger, and Gray 1991, p. 7).

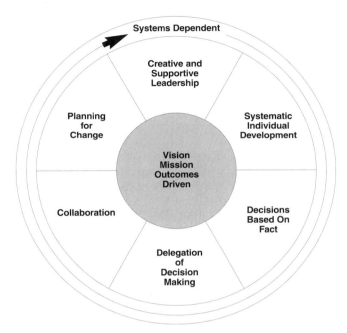

Defining an institution's vision, mission, and values is the first step in creating an empowered culture (Wellins, Byham, and Wilson 1991). A vision statement is a statement about an organization's future state. A mission statement is more specifically focused, outlines the institution's purpose, and should differentiate the institution from other institutions (Block 1989). Values are core beliefs that unite members. Vision and values must be communicated throughout the organization in a way that builds commitment and meaning. Vision is the only universal characteristic of effective leadership in the literature. Effective leaders help to establish a compelling vision, set clear standards for performance, and create a focus and direction for all organizational efforts (Bolman and Deal 1991; Pascarella and Frohman 1990).

Organizations can better reach their potential if all individuals understand and are committed to the vision, mission, and values. This shared understanding requires that the organization's purposes be highly visible and woven into its processes. The core mission becomes part of every employee's informal job description. Leaders model and communicate the mission and related values at every opportunity. The mission becomes a powerful driver for action when an institution is fully aligned with it. Sharing an organization's mission and values with every employee from the beginning helps to develop a shared sense of purpose.

Thus, a sense of ownership is instilled, and people become more personally committed to their work (Deal and Jenkins 1994). A recent study that compared the most outstanding and enduring companies in the United States with their nearest rivals found that one of the companies' most distinguishing characteristics was that their leaders had a distinctive vision and sense of mission for the organizations and that the vision and mission were clearly communicated to and internalized by every member of the organization (Porras and Collins 1994).

An organization's vision grows as a by-product of individual visions, a by-product of ongoing conversations (Senge 1990). If they are to act in ways that support the institution's mission, employees must understand the mission and what they can do to contribute to it. One common criticism of mission and vision statements is that they are written in textbook language and posted on the wall or printed in institutional publications. Although these methods can be effective, vision and mission statements, to guide behavior, must be connected to institutional values and be part of everyday performance development.

If employees are to internalize the statements, the statements must become an active part of the daily culture. Vision and mission statements must be moved from signs on the walls into employees' minds and hearts. To do so is extremely difficult but necessary, for when the mission is internalized, employees act as radio beacons of information, pulsing out information everywhere. Everyone begins stating, clarifying, discussing, and modeling the messages that are significant to the institution. Institutional members must get their "fingerprints" on the mission by sharing in its development, communicating it in as many ways as possible. When making strategic decisions for the institution, people are reminded to refer to the institutional vision and mission statements for guidance.

These statements are similar to an institutional compass, because they help indicate direction (Wheatley 1994).

Because the long-term health of any organization depends on how well the organization satisfies the needs of people being served, development and revision of the vision and mission statements starts with identifying the stakeholders. And even though it is a logical step, identifying all the stakeholders for the entire institution, assessing their needs, and involving them directly in the process is often *not* part of the culture in higher education institutions.

In the past, judgments about institutional quality were often determined by measuring resources or by assessing opinions of insiders or peers. Reputation, scores on admission tests, size of the endowment, and percentage of Ph.D.s on the faculty are still common measures of quality, largely because these indicators are quantifiable and available. The quality principles, in combination with assessment of process and outcomes, have redefined quality to go beyond how well a student tests at the end of a course to how well a student learns.

Exceeding stakeholders' expectations is what distinguishes the very successful institutions from the average. Stakeholders' expectations are based on certain standards. If the standards are met, the stakeholder is satisfied and the institution is perceived to be a quality institution. If the stakeholder sees another institution exceeding expectations, the stakeholder's institution is perceived as being of lesser quality. Monitoring the expectations of stakeholders is important, because their expectations may change based on what they value at any particular time. Changing expectations is a natural process, driven by changes in the external environment.

Most colleges and universities do not understand precisely who their stakeholders are and have even less information about how stakeholders view the institution (Seymour 1992). But without stakeholders' knowledge, the use of quality tools, techniques, and training is not enough (Sashkin and Kiser 1993). Collecting systematic data to learn about stakeholders' expectations and perceptions is a continual process (Seymour and Collett 1991). Because quality is a perception, it is important to survey stakeholders to determine what their perceptions are, for perceptions are reality to the user. "Quality is what customers say it is, not what universities tell them it is" (Coate 1990, p. 27).

Who are the stakeholders? Broadly defined, a stakeholder is anyone who can say "no" (Carothers and Richmond 1993). As the term implies, it is anyone who *holds* a *stake* in the organization's success. The literature on total quality management and continuous quality improvement uses the concepts of "external customer" and "internal customer" to cover the concept of "stakeholder" (Deming 1986; Schmidt and Finnigan 1992; Whiteley 1991). The concept of "customer" is too restrictive for nonprofit organizations, whose status has been granted to serve a social good, because a much wider range of people are concerned about or have a stake in the organization's success. The "customer" in higher education is the "beneficiary"—"the persons, group, or groups who benefit from our services" (Chaffee and Sherr 1992, p. 20). This monograph uses the term "stakeholder," because it is a more inclusive term.

Higher education has various stakeholders. Students and parents, because they financially support and receive benefits from the institution, clearly are stakeholders, and their needs and expectations should be considered. In a research institution, agencies that fund research are key stakeholders. Faculty are major stakeholders, because they not only create the main teaching environment, but also are responsible for defining and expanding the body of knowledge being taught. In higher education, therefore, stakeholders can include students, parents, alumni, faculty, administrators, staff, funding organizations, religious affiliations, and employers. And each stakeholder plays a different role in the institution's vision, mission, values, and outcomes.

Providing quality service entails two primary challenges. First, in many cases only the front-line people who directly interact with stakeholders are trained how to provide quality service. One of the quality principles is systematic development of *all* institutional members, not just front-line members, so that they are aware of and skilled in meeting stakeholders' expectations. Second, many institutions define "stakeholder" too narrowly. If stakeholders' expectations are to be fully satisfied, the term should be expanded to include stakeholders *within* an organization as well as external receivers of the product or service (Deal and Jenkins 1994). In other words, every member in an organization works to help the organization achieve its mission. Because everyone has the same overall goal, everyone should work to help the others be successful. When an organization develops this awareness of interdependency, individual members begin to see the people they interact with, especially the ones they provide direct services to, as mutual stakeholders whose expectations they must meet to be successful (Schmidt and Finnigan 1993, pp. 5–6; Whiteley 1991).

Vital to understanding that an organization's vision, mission, and outcomes are the collective whole of its stakeholders' expectations is understanding the process of interaction among stakeholders. Each contact with a stakeholder is a *moment of truth*. When stakeholders come into contact with others in the organization, regardless of their position, the stakeholder experiences the total organization, for good or bad. In a quality culture, employees understand the significance of these moments of truth. Every interaction with a member of the organization, in the minds of stakeholders, is a reflection of the organization (Carlzon 1987).

Motorola uses another concept to help members of the organization understand the significance of stakeholders. The director of planning, quality, communication, and joint venture development at Motorola University reports that all employees of the company, regardless of position, are trained so that they understand how what they do affects both internal and external stakeholders (Serritella 1995). Motorola calls this concept *line of sight,* which means that all employees must at all times have a mental connection to the stakeholder. This concept helps to align every position to the goals of creating value for stakeholders and achieving the organization's mission.

People in higher education institutions often do not understand the concepts of moment of truth and line of sight. Because "customer service training," if provided, is usually conducted for people interacting directly with external customers, the majority of institutional members are not aware of the significance of each moment of truth or each opportunity to satisfy stakeholders. Likewise, the typical institutional culture does not encourage people to understand how their positions serve stakeholders. Because of this lack of understanding, people lose sight of who the stakeholders are and how they can influence stakeholders' satisfaction with each encounter.

While this monograph says stakeholders' expectations help to define quality, it is necessary to understand that applying this approach in human development organizations, such as higher education and health care, is different from applying it in a retail store, where the short-term interests or immediate gratification of customers—"the customer is always right"— is strongly linked to stakeholders' satisfaction. When members of the organization view relationships as relationships *with* stakeholders, they are more oriented toward service. Students, like medical patients, do not always know what is in their best long-term interests (Ruben 1995a), and stakeholders' short-term satisfaction must often be subjugated to their long-term expectations. What is critical is that all parties in a higher education institution are aware of and agree with the long-term expectations. For example, a student may not be happy about heavy homework assignments (short-term satisfaction) but is really paying tuition and attending college to receive a good education (the long-term expectation and the result of the heavy homework assignments).

Another way to think about this relationship is to understand that at various times everyone in the organization is both a stakeholder and a supplier. Thus, the role of stakeholder changes, depending on the part of the stakeholder-service process in which someone is involved. A review of the dynamics of the relationship between stakeholders and service providers or suppliers notes that higher education's approach to quality is to integrate consumers' expectations with the institution's mission and outcomes (Ruben 1995a). This approach emphasizes the interdependence of being vision, mission, and outcomes driven and the changing needs and expectations of the critical stakeholders for whom these educational services are being provided.

Belmont University in Nashville includes a customer/supplier triad in its training materials to explain how the roles of customer and supplier reverse depending on the stage of the process (see figure 3). The triad depicts the relationships involved in satisfying customers and the questions that need to be asked from the perspective of both supplier and customer. The underlying point of the triad is that everyone is a stakeholder to be satisfied and that everyone has a stakeholder to satisfy. Members of Belmont University have found this triad to be valuable in helping faculty, staff, and administrators to understand their respective roles in satisfying stakeholders' expectations.

FIGURE 3

Customer/Supplier Triad

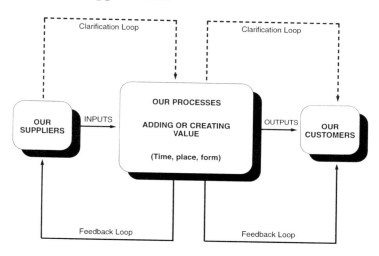

SUPPLIERS:
 Before - How can I help you do your work better?
 After - Have I given you the input you need?
CUSTOMERS:
 Before - This is what I need, when, where, how.
 After - You met/failed to meet my needs when, where, how.

Source: Belmont Univ., Center for Quality and Professional Development 1994.

The use of the word "customer" in higher education is not as successful in communicating the relationship between students and faculty as other words. When students are viewed as customers, faculty perceive themselves surrendering expertise and authority—or, as one faculty member stated, "the inmates are running the asylum" (Ewell 1993, p. 55). Although students fit some aspects of customers perfectly (in decisions concerning parking, food services, registration, and the library, for example), faculty rarely live by the maxim "the customer is always right" in the classroom. But as stakeholders in the process, students are very capable of providing valuable information about how the educational process is working for them and reporting when they are confused, bored, and/or uncertain (Bateman and Roberts 1993; Mosteller 1989).

"The biggest hurdle is to transform students into customers [stakeholders] in our own minds. As students, they belong to us; as customers [stakeholders], the learning process is mutually owned" (Seymour and Collett 1991, p. 19). Once we shift our thinking to view students as stakeholders, the emphasis is not on teaching but on learning. Faculty are the key components of the process of improving the quality of education for students. For most students, the faculty *are* the college or university, because the classroom is where students interact most often with members of the institution. Therefore, faculty members are crucial to students' perception of the institution as a quality institution.

Institutions cognizant of serving both internal and external stakeholders are practicing this quality principle. Internal stakeholders are persons or units within the organization that interact with and depend upon another person or unit within the organization for service. Academic departments, the admissions, alumni, and registrar's offices, trustees, and faculty are all internally linked. The internal process is a stream in which the quality of a product or service downstream is best assured by maintaining quality service upstream (Seymour 1992). External stakeholders include current and prospective students, current and prospective donors, parents, alumni, employers, government agencies, suppliers, and high school counselors (Corts 1992). In essence, higher education institutions serve numerous external groups, each with its own needs and expectations. Although deciding which stakeholders' needs have priority is a continual challenge, the important point to remember is that stakeholders' needs and expectations must be considered when making decisions in which they have a stake or valuable input.

Three underlying principles concerning quality service are important to academe:

1. The most important part of any organization is the people it serves.
2. To attract new stakeholders and retain old ones, their needs have to be satisfied.
3. Stakeholders' needs have to be identified to be satisfied (Chaffee and Sherr 1992).

As stakeholders change, their needs change. To serve them effectively, institutions must collect data to answer several questions: Who are the stakeholders? What are their needs? How are their needs determined? Are their needs being met?

And what determines whether their needs are being met? One tool for identifying needs is Quality Function Deployment (QFD), described as an organized system to identify and prioritize stakeholders' needs and to translate them into a college's or university's priorities. QFD correlates stakeholders' requirements with internal processes so that work is done correctly the first time, decreasing rework and increasing communication. In addition to QFD, tools like surveys of stakeholders, focus groups, and suggestion systems help to clarify stakeholders' needs and determine whether their needs are being met. The tools are useful in monitoring stakeholders' needs and expectations when they are applied systematically to collect data (Peachy and Seymour 1993).

The goal of the quality movement in education should be developing satisfied stakeholders, whether they are students, parents of students, alumni, professors, or industries (Seymour 1992). Doing so involves improving the quality of teaching and research. Parents and potential students, however, sometimes look for alternative indicators of quality, such as first-rate facilities, well-managed finances, groomed grounds, and customer-friendly administrative processes that reflect an institution's image and identity (Deal and Jenkins 1994). Therefore, in serving stakeholders, leaders must remember that quality is perceived in both internal processes and external factors.

To improve customer service:

1. Make service an institutionwide value. Service must be a priority for all.
2. Connect all departments to the vision and mission statements. The more members feel connected, the more value they assign to their contribution.
3. Require customer service training for everyone. Training can inspire a focus on stakeholders across all levels of the institution.
4. Incorporate service as a criterion for performance. Remember the maxim "Don't expect what you don't inspect" (Deal and Jenkins 1994).

All members of the institution must understand that all players and all departments depend on the interrelationships involved. Quality service is everyone's responsibility. All members must understand their roles in the system and how

All members of the institution must understand that all players and all departments depend on the interrelationships involved. Quality service is everyone's responsibility.

they positively or negatively affect stakeholders, which becomes more difficult for jobs removed from direct contact with the external stakeholders. Paying close attention to students, faculty, staff, administrators, alumni, parents, and all the other constituencies of higher education is an attitude that should permeate the entire institution. It is particularly important to monitor these stakeholders, because ultimately they define the institution's vision, mission, and outcomes. They are the people who have a personal interest in wanting the institution to succeed.

Institutions that are vision, mission, and outcomes driven understand that monitoring and including stakeholders' expectations is one of the two most important components of the quality principles, for it is the hub of the quality system. The second component is understanding that how well the perimeter of the system functions depends on how well the interrelated systems function to achieve the mission. Together, these two principles hold the other principles together and create the dynamic that makes the quality principles such a powerful and effective new paradigm.

SYSTEMS DEPENDENT

*When placed in the same system, people, however differ-
ent, tend to produce similar results* (Senge 1990, p. 42).

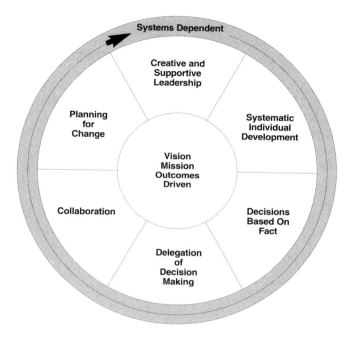

While the most important assets of an institution are its people (administrators, faculty, and staff), the overall success of
the institution depends on how well its people relate to each
other—that is, how well designed are the processes and
systems that are to achieve the institution's mission? Even
the most gifted personnel will fail if they operate in a system
that is designed to fail (Denton 1995). The solution to an
institution's challenges may be in the system that requires a
change in mind-set and helps people deal with situations
from a different perspective. From the perspective of the
system:

1. *There are few people problems.*
2. *There are only management problems.*
3. *Most management problems are systems problems* (Lytle
   1995, p. 16).

Systems analysis is not a new field. What is new is applying the concepts to organizations and institutions, which involves new ways of thinking about how work is accomplished and how to manage work tasks. The value of understanding systems is in understanding that how people function is almost always a function of the systems they have experienced. When systems are changed, behaviors change. Therefore, systems affect how people think, act, and feel. They affect the relationships within the institution that influence the culture. Systems can enhance accomplishment of an institution's mission or be major restraints.

The concept of wholeness is important in understanding systems:

- The whole should be the primary focus of analysis, with the parts receiving secondary attention.
- Integration is the key variable in understanding wholeness, defined as interrelatedness of the many parts within the whole.
- Modifications in each part should be considered in relation to possible effects on every other part.
- Each part has a role to perform so that the whole can accomplish its purpose.
- The nature of the part and its function is based on its position in the whole.
- All analysis starts with confirming the existence of the whole. The parts and their interrelationships evolve to best satisfy the purpose of the whole (Hopkins 1937).

A system is often defined as a set of parts. To be "systems dependent" means that the performance of the system depends on how the parts function as a whole. Because institutions comprise numerous parts, it is essential for all the various parts to work together to accomplish the institution's mission and outcomes, requiring a shift in thinking for people within institutions, because history has tended to reinforce the tendency of people to act independently. On the academic side, the norm is to master a discipline and teach within that area, with little overlap in other areas. Team teaching and interdisciplinary courses are relatively new concepts in higher education.

To create a quality culture in higher education requires an emphasis on viewing institutions as systems, and a systemic orientation is necessary to understand the relationships among the quality principles. A system is a whole that cannot be divided into independent parts and then function (Ackoff 1995). Its characteristics are that each part of the system affects behaviors and properties of the whole system, no part of the system has an independent effect on the whole system, and each subsystem affects the whole system.

The significance of the quality principles is in understanding them as a system. For the principles to have the greatest impact, all of them must be practiced simultaneously—the concept of *total* in total quality management. Each principle affects the whole system and is not effective as an independent principle.

Viewing organizations as systems, commonly referred to as "systems thinking," can help us understand the behavior of the people within the system (or institution or organization) and is essential in identifying the system's "leverage points." Leverage points are the places where a change made with a minimum of effort yields positive or negative results. Because the eight quality principles are to be implemented as a system, there are numerous leverage points within the institutional system where adjustments can be made. This systems orientation is the thread that weaves the quality principles together.

From an early age, we are taught to analyze situations by dividing up problems. The goal is to make complex tasks more manageable, but this approach has problems: It is difficult to see the consequences of actions and connections to the larger whole (Senge 1990). Managers should take a long-term perspective to quality, using a systems approach to improve organizational effectiveness (Crosby 1992; Deming 1986; Juran 1992). In this approach, subsystems work together for the good of the whole system. "Any group should have as its aim optimization over time of the larger system that the group operates in. Anything less than optimization of the whole system will bring eventual loss to every component in the system" (Deming 1993, p. 46).

A current approach toward understanding organizations is to see them as systems of interrelated parts, giving primary value to the relationships among the parts. The objective should not be to analyze systems by taking them apart, for when a system is taken apart, it loses its essential function. "A system is more than the sum of its parts" (Ackoff 1974, p.

13), and "system performance depends critically on how well the parts fit and work together, not merely on how well each performs when considered independently" (p. 15).

An automobile functions correctly only when the critical parts fit together. An all-star team is rarely as good as the best team in the league from which the players were selected, because it depends on how well the players work together. These examples suggest that we should "stop managing actions and start managing interaction" (Ackoff 1995). Every job in an organization is part of a process, and only by understanding the role each job plays in meeting the overall mission can the process be improved. Quality means to "improve constantly and forever every system of production and service" (Gabor 1990, p. 20).

For commercial enterprises, the trend is toward more fluid, organic organizations without boundaries. When organizations are recognized as systems, it is easier to understand how organizations possess many of the properties of living systems, such as interacting with their environment and individual parts affecting other parts. Management theory has historically referred to these types of organizations as open systems, implying that they interact with the external environment (Birnbaum 1988). Thinking in terms of systems is an important breakthrough in analyzing organizations, because it "is a framework for seeing interrelationships rather than things, for seeing patterns of change rather than static snapshots" (Senge 1990, p. 68). Systems that influence the level of quality perceived include how we do work, how we hold people accountable, how we evaluate, promote, and discipline others, and how effectively we provide services to those we serve (LeTarte 1993).

It is essential to understand the systems in an institution to be able to effect the desired outcome—quality. In a quality culture, systems based on traditional management philosophies are eliminated and replaced by a philosophy that values stakeholders and empowers members. The systems of the past are obsolete, and change is necessary to adapt to the dynamic environment. Because organizations are webs of relationships, processes and people within organizations interact continually, and a change in any aspect of the organization affects the other parts.

"Process" is an important concept in understanding systems. It shifts attention away from the results to the steps of the process producing those results. Continually improving processes through the use of tools, data collection, and support by institutional leadership reinforces the idea that the quality principles are a systematic approach.

Several metaphors can be used to understand this new organizational perspective. Organizations are like a mobile; when one part moves, all the other parts are affected. Because systems help to make order out of chaos, another applicable metaphor is that of a marching band. In a system, people understand the significance of the roles they play. Likewise in a marching band, it is only because each member understands the role that he or she plays that the entire band is able to construct a drill. At times, the audience may not be able to perceive the design, but band members have a conceptual vision of the outcome of the drill and so are able to align themselves and create an effective performance.

Another mental model is to view an organization as a theater; it takes many different people playing a variety of roles to have a successful production (Deal and Jenkins 1994). The key is to understand the interactions among all parts of the system. Actions can reinforce and balance each other. Considering the outcomes as the results of several steps and individuals working together recognizes the relationships of the process. Processes are simplified and continually improved when the focus is on meeting the mission or outcomes of the activity, whether it is teaching a class or operating a college.

In thinking about results as the product of a system, another shift takes place. Organizations have been viewed as linear when, in reality, systems are circular, indicating that all parts influence the other parts. Because organizations are relationships, "from the systems perspective, the human actor is part of the feedback process, not standing apart from it. This represents a profound shift in awareness" (Senge 1990, p. 78). The system is viewed as one where "each employee is a link in a tightly connected causal chain that determines whether the final product or service is of high or low quality" (Deal and Jenkins 1994, p. 76). Any break in the chain will affect whether the stakeholder's experience was satisfactory or unsatisfactory.

Systems analysis can be used to illustrate the circular nature and interdependence of events operating within institutions that are most often seen as separate and distinct. Figure

4, for example, illustrates several points of influence affecting a department chair's performance from the perspective of the administration. The original performance expectation for the role of the department chair is based on administrative needs and expectations, and it is assumed that everyone in the institution agrees with this definition of the role; training, evaluation, and feedback are all predicated on this administrative expectation. The result is a perception of responsibilities for the job internalized by the chair that greatly influences the quality of performance for that position.

FIGURE 4

The Role of the Department Chair from the Administration's Perspective

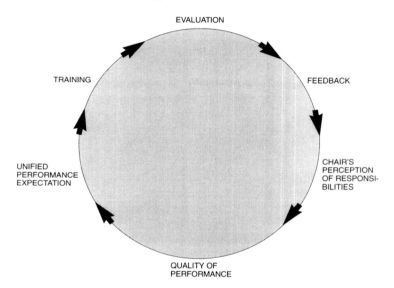

EVALUATION

TRAINING

FEEDBACK

UNIFIED
PERFORMANCE
EXPECTATION

CHAIR'S
PERCEPTION
OF RESPONSI-
BILITIES

QUALITY OF
PERFORMANCE

If, however, the department chair is elected by the faculty, a second set of expectations influences this position. Figure 5 depicts the role of the department chair from the perspective of the faculty. Here, the faculty's expectations of the department chair are developed over time and are institutionalized in a code of governance, including the selection process for the department chair and the chair's duties. These expectations in turn determine the type of training, evaluation, and feedback that occurs. The result is that faculty have a preconceived image of the role of the chair, even before he or she takes the position, and the preconceived image influences that faculty member's performance.

FIGURE 5

The Role of the Department Chair from the Faculty's Perspective

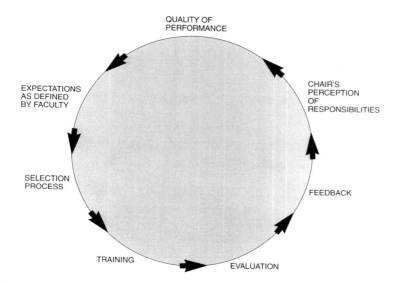

If administrators and faculty see the department chair only from their own vantage points, they miss the potential dynamics and conflict of the relationship between expectations and performance when they are seen as two interdependent systems (figure 6). When viewed from this vantage point, potential conflicts become more obvious. The first level of conflict exists if the two sets of expectations are significantly different. The second exists if training, evaluation, and feedback do not reinforce the original expectations for the role. Because, at most institutions, department chairs receive a minimal amount of training, evaluation, and feedback, the chair's perception of responsibility depends directly on the potentially conflicting expectations from administrators and faculty, producing inconsistent and hence unpredictable performance as a chair.

FIGURE 6

The Department Chair's Dilemma

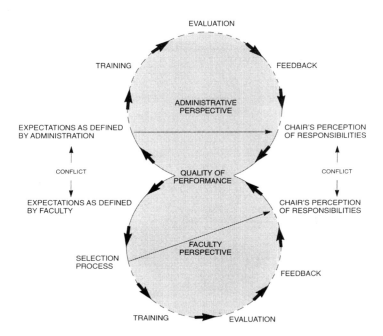

Analyzing the department chair's performance from the perspective of *the system* ensures a better chance of understanding that poor performance may be the result, not of the chair's incompetence, but perhaps of system conflicts and inconsistencies that can be corrected through expectations, training, and evaluation consistent with the values of both administrators and faculty and the institution's mission.

An examination of the admissions process shows that what looks like a series of simple decision points are really parts of several interrelated systems. Figure 7 illustrates the admissions process from an administrative perspective. First a strategy is developed to portray a distinctive institutional image, which is then translated into various forms of communication designed to create positive expectations in prospective students and distributed by the admissions office. The intended result is to motivate a student to visit the campus and then submit an application for admission and financial aid and, if accepted, enroll.

FIGURE 7

**The Admissions Process from the
Administration's Perspective**

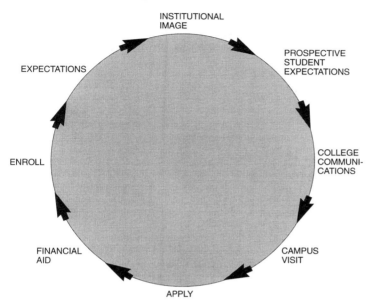

From a student's perspective, the critical points in deciding which colleges to apply to are quite different. As shown in figure 8, the first point of influence is the opinions of parents, friends, and siblings, the second is the recommendations of his or her school's guidance office and teachers, and the third is the institutions' academic and social offerings. If all these influences are positive, the student may then seek information from the institution, visit the campus, formally apply for admission and financial aid, and then enroll.

If the admissions process is viewed as incremental and independent steps, failure to see where the process may not be successful becomes more likely than when admissions is seen from the perspective of a system that includes both the admissions office and students. This system vantage point can be enhanced even more when a process is viewed as several systems connected with and dependent on each other. Figure 9 depicts the admissions process as three sets of interrelated, interdependent systems based on critical decision phases: creating interest among students, getting students to apply, and ensuring that they enroll.

FIGURE 8

The Admissions Process from Students' Perspective

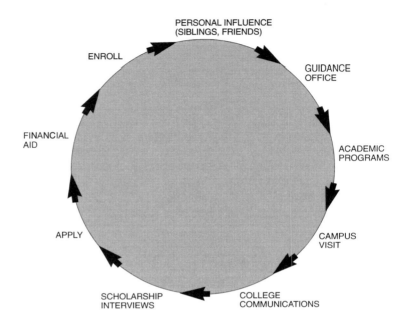

FIGURE 9

The Dilemma of the Admissions Process

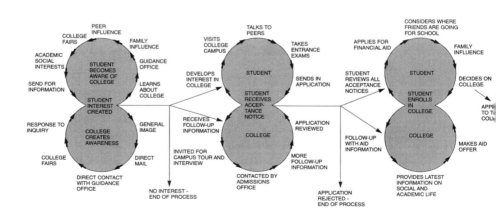

A significant advantage of breaking outcomes, such as enrolling a student, into separate systems is that it helps to understand the cause of an outcome that may be hidden deep within a subsystem. For example, in figure 9, the reason a student may fail to enroll is that he or she has an inaccurate perception about the academic quality of the institution that was created because inadequate information was provided the school's guidance office.

Systems analysis has two advantages: to understand better the influence of individual points in determining whether a certain objective will be met and to understand the roles played by various units and people in accomplishing the objective. Systems analysis leads to a type of systematic thinking that promotes inclusiveness in the implementation of planning and produces greater communication, data gathering, training, and consistency within an organization.

Systems analysis can also be useful when examining what appear to be two separate and independent systems, either one or both of which may have caused the same result. The retention of students is an example of this type of analysis. Figure 10 illustrates an administrative perspective of the retention process. If advising, programs, costs, living conditions, extracurricular activities, and social and personal experiences are acceptable, it is assumed that students will be happy and will remain at the institution until they graduate.

FIGURE 10

The Retention Process from the Administration's Perspective

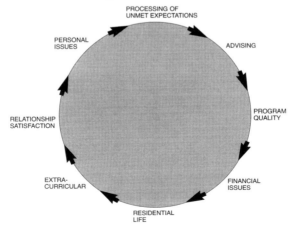

PROCESSING OF
UNMET EXPECTATIONS

PERSONAL
ISSUES

ADVISING

PROGRAM
QUALITY

RELATIONSHIP
SATISFACTION

EXTRA-
CURRICULAR

FINANCIAL
ISSUES

RESIDENTIAL
LIFE

Figure 11 shows the retention process from a student's perspective. This representation assumes that if they are satisfied with their relationships, academic programs, extracurricular activities, and costs, and if the external community is not too hostile, students will remain at the institution.

FIGURE 11

The Retention Process from Students' Perspective

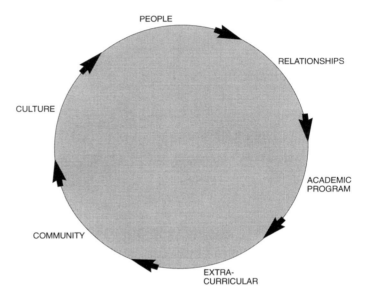

The challenges to retention, however, are not the responsibility of just one department. The challenges must be understood as cross-functional, involving all subsystems affecting and affected by the dynamics of retention. What encourages students to remain motivated to continue their studies is directly related to the integration of both an academic and a social relationship (Paulsen 1990). Figure 12 illustrates these two relationships and the influence the two systems have on a decision to remain at an institution. Systems theory emphasizes that retention is a much larger responsibility for institutional members than what is normally perceived. An institution must pay careful attention to both areas of a student's life if retention is to be assured.

As these figures illustrate, systems analysis views processes as circular. The circles may imply order, but order is not implied in the examples given. The intention is to understand the components of the process and the relationships of the parts of the system. In reality, the systems may vary from institution to institution. The value of the systems perspective is the ability to develop a conceptual framework for how the various parts are related, how the parts positively or negatively affect each other.

FIGURE 12

The Dilemma of the Retention Process

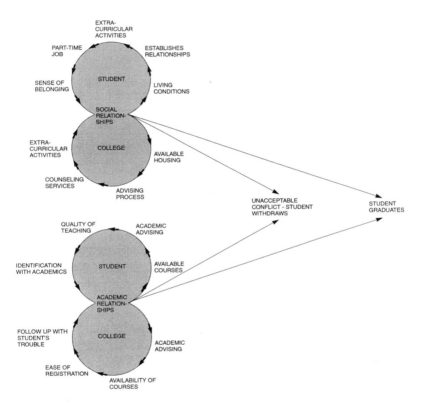

Similar systems diagrams concerning retention from the perspectives of administrators and students (figures 10 and 11, respectively) illustrate how important relationships are, not only in recruiting students, but also in retaining them. When the two systems are merged (as shown in figure 12), it becomes apparent how conflict can emerge when the same forces that influenced their choice of college play the same heartstrings and feed the sleeping homesickness giant. Students trust these influential people, and when they are separated from them, it becomes difficult for the institution to keep the students.* These examples emphasize how all the parts must work together to be effective and that each part influences the other parts. No part acts independently of the system, and any change to one part of the system's organization therefore will affect some other part of the organization.

Costs can be decreased and service to stakeholders improved by eliminating delays or duplicated processes in the system. To be effective, however, systems and processes must reflect and reinforce the institution's values. This "system congruence" (Wellins, Byham, and Wilson 1991) occurs when all the systems work together to accomplish and support the institution's mission and values. One role of management is to define and design systems that build in quality, where employees have a role to continuously revise, refine, and redesign work processes in the institution to maintain and improve quality (Sashkin and Kiser 1993).

The paradigm of understanding the parts of a higher education institution as discrete, incremental, and chronological has changed to seeing them as a continuous, interdependent, and interrelated whole. Thinking of the parts as a system integrates all the quality principles. The system in a quality culture is designed so the institution can accomplish its mission and outcomes as defined by stakeholders. All of the systems—including leadership, development, data collection, decision making, collaboration, and planning for change—and related subsystems—such as recruitment and selection, communication, and rewards—must be designed to be congruent with each other, and the supporting philosophy must be one of continuous improvement (Neal and Tromley 1995). Once a systems orientation is the context in which problems are solved, an institution's use of quality tools and techniques to collect data for the purpose of improving the system will be successful. Being systems dependent involves a change in the institutional culture. This principle must be consistently practiced because it integrates all the other principles.

---

*Eric Sickler 1995, personal communication.

Top leaders play crucial roles in changing the culture of an institution. They align members to the institution's vision, mission, and outcomes. Their commitment to quality improvement, demonstrated through their actions, behaviors, and attitudes, inspires others. As leaders "talk the talk" and "walk the talk," the culture begins to change. Strong leadership drives the quality principles by creating the culture early in the journey toward quality and supporting efforts toward continuous improvement continually along the journey (see "Creative and Supportive Leadership"). If they are to engage in the quality principles, members need to develop the knowledge and skills necessary to improve processes and systems and to make the quality principles a personal philosophy for thinking, feeling, and behaving.

SYSTEMATIC INDIVIDUAL DEVELOPMENT

I know of no institution in our society that does a poorer job of educating its own employees than higher education (Lawrence Sherr, cited in Seymour 1992, p. 104).

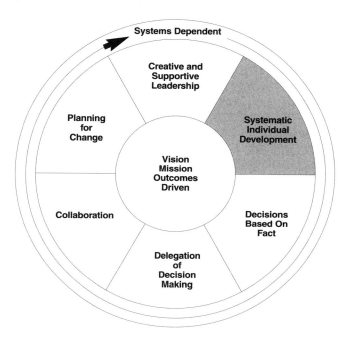

The actions of senior leaders reflect their ideas about empowerment and continuous improvement. When they are serious about empowerment and continuous improvement, senior leaders commit time and resources to developing the required knowledge and skills in all members of the organization. Education and training are essential to transform institutions, and the responsibility to invest in human resources rests with senior leaders. "Unless you take care of the human side of quality, you will never realize the true benefits of a quality organization" (Thor 1993, p. 2). Management must begin by making continual self-improvement a priority and by accepting the responsibility for continuous training of people in the organization.

Although it is difficult to determine how much time and money should be spent on training, some researchers have discovered that organizations actively practicing the quality principles have employees spend a minimum of about 40 hours in training for the first year (Brown, Hitchcock, and Willard 1994). The training is usually divided into three phases: (1) the concept of quality (eight to 12 hours), (2) tools (16 to 24 hours), and (3) special topics (four to 16 hours). In subsequent years, about 16 to 32 hours of additional training is necessary. Even though this model is only one of many identified in the literature (see, e.g., O'Brien, McEachern, and Luther 1996; Tucker 1993), it emphasizes that members of an organization must be educated about the philosophy of the quality principles if they are to be fully engaged in the search for quality.

Managers need leadership training to develop skills of coaching, facilitating, and empowering. Until recently, most efforts to apply the quality principles focused on administrative operations, and most training and education was targeted more toward the administration and staff and less toward the faculty, because administrative practices more closely reflect business practices and because quality improvement originated in business and industry. Support staff most frequently receive training (89 percent of responding institutions in one survey), followed by administration (85 percent) and then faculty (67 percent) (Freed, Klugman, and Fife 1994). While the quality movement places a high priority on training employees at all levels, educating faculty as well as administration and staff is central to the cultural transformation.

In a culture subscribing to quality improvement, the traditional, passive faculty development committee is being replaced by professional and personal development committees for both faculty and staff. The primary focus is on how everyone served can receive the highest quality education possible, and it involves ongoing training in which employees at all levels have access to workshops, seminars, and courses related to quality. One of the most important results of training in the quality principles is the development of an internal common language that allows effective communication (Cornesky et al. 1992).

While it is necessary that top leaders be committed to the process, it is equally important to train all the leaders to "walk the talk." A common model of development usually has two main phases. The first phase is an introduction to the quality concepts, which includes communication skills, problem-solving techniques, customer service, and team building.

Employees are introduced to measurement, charting, and costing. They begin to apply statistical analysis and to use control systems. The second phase involves more specific training for individual groups. Some institutions use just-in-time training so members are trained for when they need specific skills. Customer service is emphasized throughout the training sessions, because all employees need to learn how to listen to customers and to solve problems (Cocheu 1993).

Faculty members often become trainers in the learning process, which gives them new roles. This change helps structures to become less hierarchical. New titles are created, and revised systems challenge traditional systems (Spanbauer 1992). Fifty-two percent of the institutions implementing the quality principles in one survey use a combination of staff trainers, faculty trainers, and outside consultants (Freed, Klugman, and Fife 1994), reinforcing the fact that having internal personnel conduct training is important in demonstrating an institution's commitment to quality.

Training needs to be part of the system so that it is a continuing way of life for all members of higher education.

Organizations are quick to blame workers for problems with quality when the problems most likely are caused by a lack of in-depth training and inadequate design of the system (Deming 1986). Training needs to be part of the system so that it is a continuing way of life for all members of higher education. A solid commitment of resources is necessary to transform institutions into learning organizations—although an organization full of learners does not add up to a learning organization (Marchese 1993).

Ironically, the primary function of colleges and universities is the development of students, yet faculty and staff development is often a low priority (Winter 1991). "For an organization whose very existence is based on the need for education, it is amazing that universities pay so little attention to training their own employees" (Bonser 1992, p. 510). Because they lack training, administrators often make decisions without collecting the necessary data or consulting the appropriate people. Many faculty members do not collect data from students when they make improvements for students. "Where else could the idea of a culture oriented [toward] continuous improvement be more appropriate than in institutions whose primary purpose is to support improvement and individual growth?" (Gore 1993, p. 355).

Systematic individual development through continuous education and training is necessary if institutions are ready to address the one constant of organizational survival: being able to meet stakeholders' changing expectations. To do so, institutions must make decisions based on data systematically collected from stakeholders.

If you can't measure something, you can't understand it; if you can't understand it, you can't control it; if you can't control it, you can't improve it (Harrington 1987, p. 103).

In God we trust. All others must use data (W. Edwards Deming, cited in Walton 1986, p. 96).

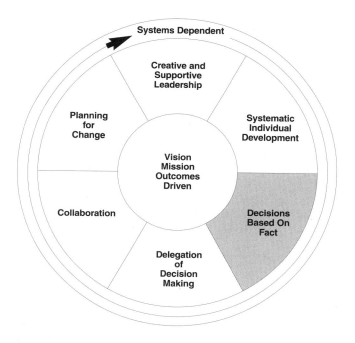

Higher education institutions must monitor the quality of the goods and services they provide to be able to improve continuously—which means that people in those organizations must systematically keep track of how the organization is doing and that the resulting information must be readily available to all within the organization. Decisions in higher education often have been made or influenced by personal impression, anecdote, or complaint. Instead, the quality principle "decisions based on fact" urges higher education to "keep track, dig out the facts, find the systemic problem or root cause" (Marchese 1993, p. 12), and concentrate on it to improve the organization. Data collection is also associated with assessment in higher education. Institutions involved in assessment have stated outcomes and key indicators of undergraduate education and have collected data over time. The movement toward quality elevates the use of data to another level: "What is the point of the assessor's 'knowledge for improvement' if continuous improvement isn't the aim?" (Marchese 1993, p. 12).

Quality improvement can be described with 10 questions or steps:

1. *What do I or we want to accomplish? (Identify mission.)*
2. *Who cares and what do they care about? (Identify stakeholders and requirements.)*
3. *What are we doing now and how well are we doing it? (Assess current state; develop a baseline.)*
4. *What can we do better? (Define preferred state, problems, and improvement opportunities.)*
5. *What prevents us from doing better? (Identify barriers and root causes.)*
6. *What changes could we make to do better? (Develop improvement solutions, strategies, tactics, and plans.)*
7. *Do it. (Implement plans.)*
8. *How did we do? If it didn't work, try again. (Monitor results; recycle if necessary.)*
9. *If it worked, how can we do it every time? (Standardize.)*
10. *What did we learn? Let's celebrate! (Conclude project.)*
(Tague 1995, p. 12).

These 10 steps are an elaboration of the Plan-Do-Check-Act cycle originally proposed by Walter A. Shewhart in the 1930s and taught in Japan by Deming (Deming 1986). They offer a systematic or scientific method for continuous quality improvement. Figure 13 shows the sequence of working through the steps. Often, an organization does not proceed smoothly from the first step to the last but may need to go back to an earlier step when a change does not work or may need to begin work on another change. Measurement and data collection are critical in every quality improvement process, and the flow chart in figure 13 indicates which steps of the process involve measurement.*

---

*See Ruben 1995a for a simplified version of this process for higher education, which includes six steps: determine/review mission and vision, assess expectations, assess performance, identify gaps, plan improvements, and integrate changes.

FIGURE 13

Flow Chart of the Quality Improvement Process

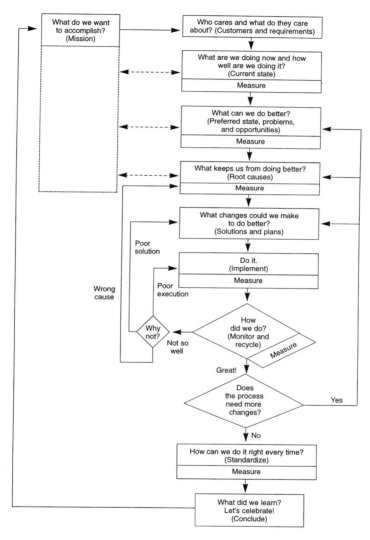

Source: Tague 1995, p. 13.

A tendency exists to equate quality with tools, which turns the focus inward to the institution's internal processes. Several tools are useful in continuous improvement, but they are the means and not the end of continuous improvement. If use of the tools leads to improvements in products and services that stakeholders do not want, the efforts have not accomplished the goal. When the focus is on the tools instead of meeting or exceeding stakeholders' expectations, the results will likely not be the desired ones. "Paradigm shifts do not often come as a result of using quality tools[, but] the tools can help one understand the data and the need for a paradigm shift" (Law 1993, p. 24).

Tools are essential for implementing the quality principles; they make it possible to collect, visualize, analyze, and interpret information to improve a process. Many tools are available for these purposes; some are useful for interpreting numerical data, while others can be applied to verbal data. The importance of the tools used for numerical data is to teach the meaning of variability and to have people learn to control it (Sashkin and Kiser 1993). The tools used for verbal data help organize issues, ideas, and words rather than numbers (Brassard 1989).*

The appropriateness of a particular tool depends on how it is to be used and at what stage it is to be used in quality improvement. Six categories of tools have been identified according to use (see table 5):

1. Idea creation tools, used to generate new ideas or to organize many ideas;
2. Process analysis tools, used to understand a process or a part of it;
3. Cause analysis tools, used to discover the cause of a problem or situation;
4. Planning tools;
5. Evaluation tools, used to narrow a group of choices to the best one or to evaluate how well something has been done; and
6. Data collection and analysis tools (Tague 1995).

---

*For coverage of many of the quality tools, see Brassard 1989, GOAL/QPC 1988, and Tague 1995.

TABLE 5

Examples of Quality Tools

Tool category	Examples of tools
Idea creation tools	Affinity diagram, nominal group process, relations diagram
Process analysis tools	Flow chart, matrix diagram, relations diagram
Cause analysis tools	Cause-and-effect diagram, force field analysis, matrix diagram, Pareto diagram, scatter diagram, systematic diagram
Planning tools	Flow chart, force field analysis, matrix diagram, operational definitions, relations diagram, systematic diagram
Evaluation tools	Scenario builder, matrix diagram
Data collection and analysis tools	Control chart, histogram, operational definition, Pareto chart, run chart, scatter diagram

Some tools are used more frequently than others. Respondents to one survey (Freed, Klugman, and Fife 1994) were asked to rank the top three tools used in their institutions, out of 14 tools listed (affinity diagram, cause-and-effect diagram, control chart, flow chart, force field analysis, histogram, nominal group process, operational definition, Pareto diagram, relations diagram, run chart, scatter diagram, scenario builder, and systematic diagram). The list is by no means exhaustive, but the results convey both the frequency of use and the overall importance of specific tools. The top five tools indicated by the respondents in order of importance were flow chart, cause-and-effect diagram, nominal group process, affinity diagram, and Pareto diagram, all of which are easily used and typically are employed early in the analysis of processes.

Flow Chart

A flow chart is a picture of the separate steps of a process in sequential order. Such steps might include actions that must be performed, materials or services entering or leaving the process, decisions that must be made, and people who become involved. A flow chart can be used as a process analysis tool or as a planning tool. It should be used when a team

FIGURE 14

Flow Chart of the Payroll Process

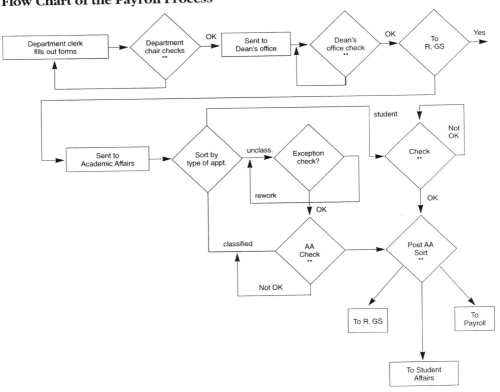

```
*    =  attachments, funding, appointment data
**   =  same as * plus signatures
AA   =  Academic Affairs
R    =  Registrar
GS   =  Graduate School
```

Source: Seymour 1992, p. 88.

begins to study a process (the first and most important step in understanding the process and finding potential areas for improvement), when an improved process is designed, when a project is planned, and when better communication is needed between people involved with the same process (Tague 1995). Figure 13 (p. 87) shows a flow chart of the 10-step quality improvement process (Tague 1995, p. 72). Note that an institution may proceed sequentially from step 1 through step 10; however, the diagram has many loops and institutions typically pass through several of the steps more than once when working to effect a particular change.

The flow chart in figure 14 was used to study a payroll process for new appointments that was experiencing many errors and complaints. Hundreds of new appointment transactions were initiated monthly, but reliable lists of the names of all appointments could not be found. Fifty percent of the forms were incompletely or incorrectly filled out. Ninety percent of these problems could be corrected by making a phone call, but the rest had to be sent back to the departments to reinitiate the process. Some of those involved in the process constructed a flow chart of the process, from which they discovered that, depending on where the transaction began in the organization, the current process required three to seven signatures. The many required signatures added cost but no value to the process.

When the signatures were eliminated as an experiment, the number of errors decreased and the time for an appointment form to reach the payroll office was reduced by 48 hours (Sherr and Lozier 1991). In this case, the flow chart made it possible to see where in the process unnecessary steps occurred, to eliminate those steps, and to end with a trimmed process that could be negotiated much more smoothly and with significantly fewer problems.

In another example, Biology 106, Anatomy and Physiology, is a service course offered by the Department of Biological Sciences as part of the School of Nursing curriculum at Samford University. The School of Nursing monitors the course through use of the National League of Nurses (NLN) board exam for anatomy and physiology (AP). Displeased by the number of students who did poorly in the course (received a grade below C), the mastery base of the C students, and the students' performance on the NLN AP exam, a team comprising the professor who taught the course, the chair of Biolog-

FIGURE 15

Flow Chart of the Original AP Process

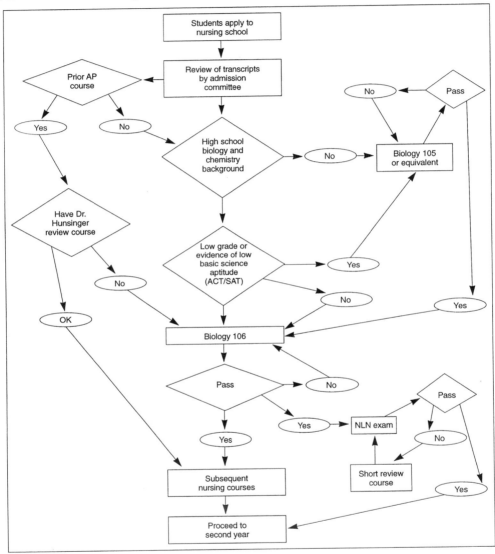

Source: Hunsinger 1992, p. 108.

ical Sciences, the dean of the School of Nursing, and the
chairs of the School of Nursing's curriculum and admissions
committees was formed to deal with the problems. By making
a flow chart of the existing process (figure 15), the team
found the process that had been in place for years had students begin by taking Biology 106 if they came to Samford

FIGURE 16

Flow Chart of the Redesigned AP Process

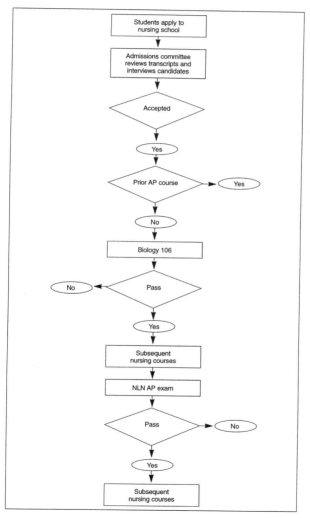

Source: Hunsinger 1992, p. 111.

with no previous AP course. When they passed Biology 106, they took additional nursing courses, after which they took the NLN AP exam. When they passed the NLN exam, they continued taking additional courses in the program.

The team saw several problems with that process and were able to incorporate suggestions for improvement into a new, redesigned process (figure 16), which included the department chair's review of AP courses from other institutions and a decision as to whether students who had taken an AP course at another institution needed to take Biology

FIGURE 17

Cause-and-Effect Diagram for Causes of Fear in the Classroom

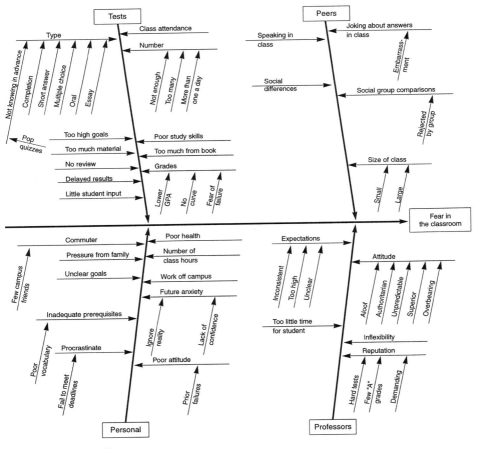

Source: Teal 1992, p. 153.

106. For students entering the system immediately out of high school, the process now included a review of the high school background and basic science aptitude test scores, followed by a decision about whether the student could enter directly Biology 106 or should first take a lower-level

FIGURE 18

Cause-and-Effect Diagram for Declining Summer School Enrollments

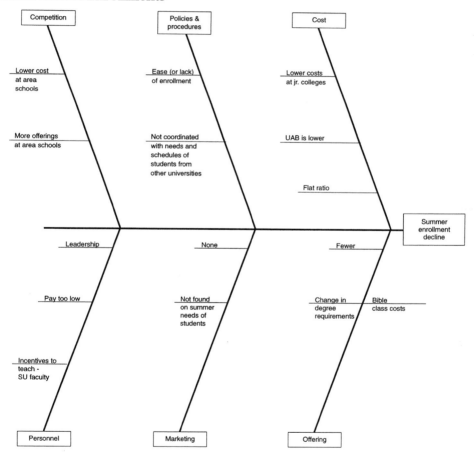

Source: Strickland and Schooley 1993, p. 9.

biology course. Finally, the team decided the NLN AP exam should be given shortly after the completion of Biology 106 to receive more immediate feedback on how well prepared students were for the remainder of the nursing curriculum (Hunsinger 1992). In this case, the flow chart of the existing process showed shortcomings in that process that could be eliminated with a redesigned process.

Cause-and-Effect Diagram

The second most important tool used among responding higher education institutions was the cause-and-effect diagram (Freed, Klugman, and Fife 1994). This tool captures,

FIGURE 19

Affinity Diagram Developed by the Advisory Committee for the Deanship

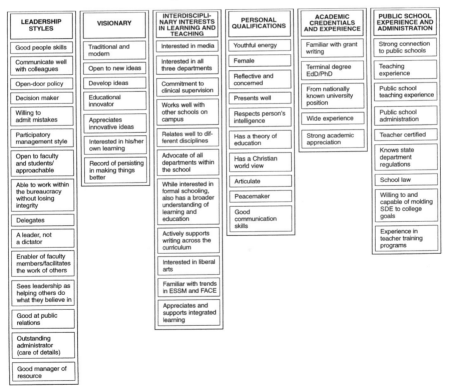

Source: Strickland and Schooley 1993, p. 7.

displays, and classifies various theories about the causes of a problem. Developed by Kaoru Ishikawa in 1943, it is often called an Ishikawa diagram or a fishbone diagram. Because it can sort ideas into useful categories, it is a good tool to bring structure to a brainstorming session. The process of drawing a cause-and-effect diagram should begin with the problem (or with the desired result) and the five generic categories for the causes: machines and equipment, materials, methods, people, and the environment. Team members often question the need for discussion of possible causes because they think that the causes are obvious, but each person sees the problem from an individual vantage point and may have his or her own ideas about possible causes (Plsek 1990).

Figure 17 is a cause-and-effect diagram about the causes of fear in the classroom. As a class project, students enrolled in a psychology course at Samford University studied the subject, conducting informal interviews with fellow students about what caused and increased fear. The students constructed a cause-and-effect diagram, grouping the causes of fear under four main headings: tests, personal causes, peers, and professors. "Tests" included type and number of tests, amount of material covered, assignment of grades, and poor study skills. "Personal causes" included students' health, number of class hours, number of work hours, procrastination, and a poor attitude about the course. "Peers" included social differences, social group comparisons, and being made fun of in class. "Professors" included their setting expectations too high, having a poor attitude toward the students, not making time for students, and being inflexible (Teal 1992). The diagram is instructive for both students and professors on a variety of situations that could be analyzed and changed to reduce fear in the classroom.

A task force formed to identify causes of declining enrollments in summer school developed the cause-and-effect diagram shown in figure 18. The task force grouped possible causes into six areas: competition with area schools, policies and procedures, cost of courses, personnel, marketing, and course offerings. From these causes, team members were able to identify actions that might lead to solutions. Every member of the team was assigned a specific task at the end of the first meeting, such as gathering data to compare costs with competing institutions in the region, identifying nontraditional times for summer courses, or exploring the possibility of an innovative tuition structure for summer school students. The cause-and-effect diagram helped to focus discussions during team meetings and to make clearer exactly what actions would be helpful in developing an action plan to solve the problem (Strickland and Schooley 1993).

Nominal Group Process and Affinity Diagram

The third most important tool, nominal group process, is a structured method for group brainstorming that encourages contributions from everyone. After the problem is stated, each team member writes down as many ideas as possible for a set period of time, and then each member states one idea aloud in turn. After all ideas have been voiced, the ideas are clarified or combined. This tool should be used when some members of the team are much more vocal than others, when some team members think better in silence, when some members may not participate in a regular brainstorming activity, when a team does not generate quantities of ideas, when the team has new members, when the issue is controversial, or when there is conflict among the team members (Tague 1995). Information for the cause-and-effect diagram in figure 18 and for the affinity diagram in figure 19 came from group brainstorming sessions.

The affinity diagram and nominal group process are both classified as "idea creation tools." Use of the affinity diagram typically follows a brainstorming or nominal group process session. It is most convenient if ideas from such a session have been recorded on stick-up notes or note cards. The notes are then spread randomly on a table, on the floor, or on the wall so that everyone can see all of them. Working quickly and in silence, each team member looks for notes that seem to be related and places them together; the team keeps working until all cards have been placed into six to 10 groups. Cards that do not seem to fit should be left to one side. During the grouping, cards may be moved several times. When the cards are grouped, the team selects a heading for each group that has been formed by using a card from the group or by making a new one (Strickland and Schooley 1993).

The advisory committee for the School of Education at Samford University used brainstorming and an affinity diagram to develop and organize a list of desirable qualities in a new dean. Instead of beginning the search for a new dean by using the usual procedure of looking for someone who had excelled as a professor and had written articles or books

FIGURE 20

Pareto Diagram of Reasons Students Scored Poorly on the NLN AP Exam

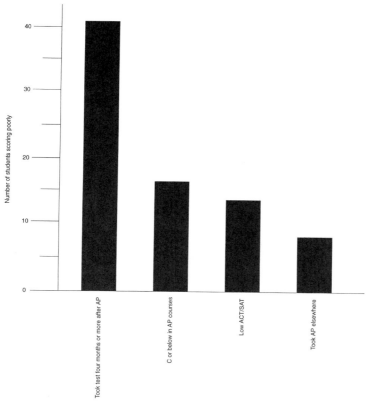

Source: Hunsinger 1992, p. 109.

in the field, the committee brainstormed to determine the characteristics they would like to see in the new dean. The affinity diagram in figure 19 was developed as a result of this exercise. The six categories that emerged from the brain-storming were leadership style, reputation as a visionary, interdisciplinary interests in learning and teaching, personal qualifications, academic credentials and experience, and public school experience and administration. The profile that resulted from this meeting was used throughout the selection process, first as criteria for advertising the position and later to rank the top choices (Strickland and Schooley 1993). In this case, the affinity diagram gave focus to chaos and provided creative input to the process of hiring a new dean.

FIGURE 21

Pareto Diagram for Causes of Fear in the Classroom

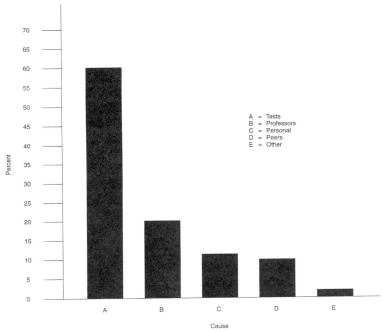

Source: Teal 1992, p. 152.

Pareto Diagram

The Pareto diagram, categorized as both a "cause analysis tool" and a "data collection and analysis tool" (Tague 1995) was the fifth most important tool cited in the survey (Freed, Klugman, and Fife 1994). The Pareto principle comes from an Italian mathematician who discovered that, almost always, 20 percent of a process creates 80 percent of the results or, put another way, "80 percent of the problem can be attributed to 20 percent of the causes" (Omachonu and Ross 1994, p. 240). In the 1950s, Joseph Juran applied the Pareto principle to problems involving quality. He suggested that whenever a number of individual factors contribute to some overall effect, relatively few of those items (the vital few) account for the majority of the effect. In problems involving quality, a team can make noticeable improvements by focusing on the vital few.

Pareto diagrams are a type of bar chart in which the various factors that contribute to some overall effect are arranged in order from the most frequent to the least frequent. This tool can be used to reveal unnoticed patterns when data are analyzed by groups, to focus on the most significant problem or cause, to improve communication about information, and to evaluate improvement by comparisons of before and after (Tague 1995).

A Pareto diagram was constructed to determine why students did poorly on the NLN Anatomy and Physiology exam (figure 20). From the data collected on the students who did poorly on the exam, the possible reason that occurred most frequently was that they had taken the exam four or more months after taking the AP course. Other factors occurred with decreasing frequency: a student earned a C or lower in the AP course, had a low ACT or SAT score, indicating a poor aptitude for science, or took an AP course at another school. Once this information was known, team members could suggest ways to improve students' scores. Several of these suggestions were incorporated into the redesigned process (see the flow chart in figure 16): The NLN AP exam was given at the end of the AP course, admissions standards were increased, and prerequisites were established for the AP course. The Pareto diagram identified reasons for poor scores that helped to focus the ideas for improving the process (Hunsinger 1992).

Figure 21 is a Pareto diagram showing causes of fear in the classroom. After students in the psychology class at Samford University had interviewed other students about what causes or enhances fear in the classroom, they grouped the reasons and counted the number of reasons falling under each main heading (tests, personal, peers, and professors). What this small study found was that most fears in the classroom are generated by tests, followed by professors; other sources accounted for a relatively small percent of the reports (Teal 1992). This diagram makes it obvious that testing must be studied if students' fears are to be lessened.

Even though tools have been used successfully to improve processes in higher education institutions, it must be constantly remembered that the tools are simply a means to an end, not the end in themselves. The use of tools and techniques is the most visible evidence that an organization is concerned about outcomes or quality; it is also the most superficial indicator of a quality environment and therefore cannot be relied on to distinguish an organization that is practicing the quality principles from one that is not. Tools by themselves cannot lead to quality (Sashkin and Kiser 1993).

Systematically collecting data and using quality tools are not parts of the culture in most higher education institutions. Making decisions intuitively rather than on data tends to be more ingrained. In a quality culture, decisions are made based on fact.

If an institution is to react quickly to environmental changes and continuously improve quality for the people it serves, employees must be more accountable and have more authority and information. Employees need to assume more responsibility and exercise more initiative. People at all levels must be empowered to make decisions and take action.

DELEGATION OF DECISION MAKING

The person doing the job knows far better than anyone else the best way of doing the job and therefore is the one person best fitted to improve it (Waterman 1987, p. 74).

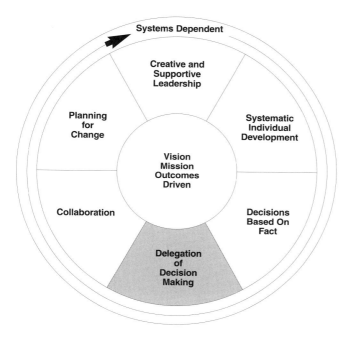

People who work within the system have the most insight into how the system works and how to improve it. The *system* must be held accountable for accomplishing measurable outcomes, and people must be committed to achieving those outcomes. This line of thinking is more common on the administrative side of the institution; the faculty's accountability for institutional goals is a rather weak concept.

Faculty members are often faulted for being too independent and too empowered. They are criticized for acting like individuals rather than members of a collective whole. The difference lies in involving and empowering them to make decisions and to hold them accountable for measurable outcomes.

If institutions are to react quickly to the imminent changes in the environment, administrators have to "put more and more accountability, authority, and information into the hands of the people who are closest to the products and customers" (Howard 1990, p. 134). "The practice of empowerment—or instilling a sense of power—is at the root of organizational effectiveness, especially during times of transition and transformation" (Conger 1989, p. 17). Empowerment enables people to take personal responsibility for and ownership of the tasks they perform (Shulman and Luechauer 1993). It should not be viewed as an end in itself but as a means of fulfilling the organization's vision (Ewell 1993; Helton 1993).

The people who can solve many of the problems affecting quality already exist within the institution. Personnel dealing with operations know more about needed daily improvements in quality than upper administrators. National retail department store Nordstrom's written philosophy states:

> *We also encourage you to present your own ideas. Your buyers have a great deal of autonomy, and are encouraged to seek out and promote new fashion directions at all times. . . . Nordstrom has a strong open-door policy, and we encourage you to share your concerns, suggestions, and ideas. . . .*
> *Nordstrom Rules:*
> *Rule #1: Use your good judgment in all situations.*
> *There will be no additional rules* (Pfeffer 1995, p. 60).

When employees are not empowered and their knowledge is not tapped, it becomes a source of frustration representing a large cost to organizations (Leffel, Robinson, Harshberger, Krallman, and Frary 1991). In a recent survey of a major university, employees reported feeling a lack of empowerment; no sense of appreciation for their efforts; little understanding of the university's policies, goals, and priorities; and almost no opportunity for professional growth. And this pattern tends to be the rule rather than the exception at colleges and universities (Deal and Jenkins 1994).

The paradox of empowerment is that "empowerment means letting go while taking control" (Baker 1994, p. 62) or gaining control by giving up control (Waterman 1987). In reality, empowering managers do not lose their powers and responsibilities; they redefine and share them (Chaffee and Seymour 1991). There is no shortage of power, for power can be given away without losing it and gained by giving it to others (Thor 1993). "Effective leaders know that one gains far more control by empowering others, [by] giving away one's formal authority" (Sashkin and Kiser 1993, p. 87). Research indicates that allowing employees to participate and become more involved increases both satisfaction and productivity (Levine and Tyson 1990).

The traditional assumption is that managers are the ones in control. The role of a manager in an empowered organization is to clear away the obstacles to effective action. According to Robert Haas, CEO of Levi Strauss and Company, empowerment is not easy:

It has been difficult for me to accept the fact that I don't have to be the smartest guy on the block—reading every memo and signing off on every decision. In reality, the more you establish parameters and encourage people to take initiatives within those boundaries, the more you multiply your own effectiveness by the effectiveness of other people (Howard 1990, p. 135).

But giving people the authority to make decisions does not mean they will make good decisions or that their actions will be effective. Employees need to be trained in the quality principles, their applications, and the statistical tools that can be used to improve quality. They need to learn how to work in teams (Sashkin and Kiser 1993). Training and education not only improves skills, but also helps employees develop an understanding of the organization. "Employees who are enabled and empowered have the knowledge, skills, and opportunity to take corrective actions to solve problems and make improvements" (p. 86).

An empowered workforce is developed by directed autonomy (Waterman 1987): All members of the organization are empowered to do things their way within a context of direction. People must know the boundaries: where and when they should act on their own, and where and when not. The manager's role is to establish those boundaries and then to get out of the way, trusting employees' judgment. Empowerment is the process of self-control and self-management (Juran 1989). Self-management can be viewed on a continuum of participative decisions (Manz and Sims 1980). Managers must make decisions about how much self-management to encourage in subordinate employees, and some criteria must be available to help make that decision

(Maier 1970; Vroom and Yetton 1973). In general, more participative decision making is appropriate when: (1) the problem is not highly structured; (2) information is needed from subordinates; (3) the solutions must be accepted by subordinates for implementation; and (4) subordinates share in the organization's goals (Manz and Sims 1980).

If they are to participate in decision making, subordinates must be fully involved. To best involve employees, four elements should be present: information, knowledge, power, and rewards. If one of the elements does not exist, employees will not get involved and will not be empowered (Lawler 1992). An individual without information cannot take responsibility, but an individual who is given information cannot help but take responsibility. Individuals who are given information, knowledge, and authority feel a sense of accomplishment, which is itself an intrinsic reward (Carlzon 1987). Leaders must be aware of all these elements to maximize employees' involvement.

Middle managers (in higher education institutions, department and division chairs or deans) are often perceived as having difficulty letting go of power. They often feel threatened when asked to share power, and they are accused of resisting change. But letting go of power may not be the only obstacle for empowering others. Department chairs, for example, are often confused about their role and have only limited power themselves (Martin 1992). One solution is to redefine the role of department and division chairs so they are an integral part of efforts to improve quality and empower them so they have power to give to others. Doing so could be accomplished by holding them accountable for their areas in contributing to the success of the whole system, not just their specific departments or divisions.

As companies become more horizontally structured, often referred to as "boundary-less," they set varying parameters for different individuals. The latitude for setting boundaries is based on experience, skills, and a proven track record. Middle managers are given power to set direction and negotiate goals for their areas within the larger system. In addition, they have the power to change processes to improve the system. "If quality is going to become a permanent part of the way we operate, middle managers must be given the power and the accountability their vital role demands" (Martin 1992, p. 90). A common mistake is bypassing middle managers in forming teams among front-line employees; in doing so, middle managers feel threatened and so do not give employees the support they need (Walton 1990).

People can feel empowered only if the environment is supportive. An empowering environment requires information to be shared that previously was considered confidential—financial information, for example. Empowering leaders hold informal gatherings of small groups to discuss company issues openly. Open communication is reinforced through organizational newsletters or electronic mail to address employees' questions and concerns. Information about objectives, measures, and rewards is shared to promote cooperation and synergy.

These efforts are supportive only if employees perceive the culture as fair. Empowering others and establishing an environment of fairness involve many of the same conditions: developing trust, acting consistently, being truthful, demonstrating integrity, clarifying expectations, treating people equitably, allowing employees to have influence, establishing just standards, and demonstrating respect (Sashkin and Kiser 1993). Fairness is important for a quality culture, because if fairness is not part of the mix, "it is difficult if not impossible for employees to feel empowered, to believe that there will be rewards for results, or to act cooperatively" (p. 105).

In an empowering culture, the reward system is structured with an emphasis on collective performance and cooperation. Because empowerment allows people at lower levels in the institution to have more responsibility and the freedom to exercise it, employees need fewer approvals and have more autonomy in making decisions. Employees must trust and respect each other to get the job done, because there is less supervision and more reliance on cooperation.

An empowering environment allows members to flourish on the job, to exercise self-control, and to provide quality service. Not only do they psychologically own their jobs, but members also have a broader perspective of work processes so they are able to catch errors and make improvements (Lawler 1992). Empowered employees need:

- Information (training and education, data, technical knowledge);
- Resources (funds, materials, space, time); and
- Support (authority, approval, legitimacy) (Kanter 1983).

In a quality culture, leaders understand how to empower others and how to build a supportive culture. People at all levels are resocialized around the new values and trained about the new boundaries. Empowerment is possible when the senior leaders in the organization learn to live in the paradox of empowerment, gaining control by giving up control, to thrive on its contradictions. To do so, some institutions are establishing learning centers or training institutes where the skills needed to function in the new environment are taught.

Empowerment can be better illustrated by an example based on studies of young children in an unfenced playground. Results have indicated that when no fence exists, children tend to stay close to the middle because they feel safer huddled together. In a playground with a fence around it, children go to the edges and explore. The role of senior leaders is to set the boundaries (the fence) and define the work environment with plenty of room to operate. Decision making should be pushed back to the appropriate level; by delegating decision making in this way, senior leaders have time to think about the boundaries (where the fence should be) and to make plans accordingly. The role of middle managers is to take the institution to the boundaries. It is their responsibility to look for broken fence posts and to suggest where the fence should be. And they are responsible for making sure the fence is safe and well maintained. In essence, middle managers safeguard the environment (Thor 1993).

Organizations, like theaters, need to spotlight more than the stars. This hidden cast of people behind the scenes is a powerful resource. When backstage contributions are respected and recognized, these unseen people respond with hard work, loyalty, dedication, and a commitment to an excellent performance. The hidden cast often feels neglected, frequently does not receive the feedback it deserves, and therefore does not understand the purpose or impact of its position to the entire production (Deal and Jenkins 1994).

A primary focus of the philosophy of quality is the empowerment of the individual:

The lesson is that we have to empower all our people with dignity, knowledge, and skills so that they [can] contribute. They have to be made secure so that they can contribute, trained so that they can do the work properly, and encouraged to grow so that the firm can develop and grow. The purpose of all of management, the purpose of cooperation, is to bring out the best in each of us and allow each of us to contribute fully (Aguayo 1990, p. 243).

Making it possible and worthwhile for employees to be committed and involved applies to the institutional culture as well—everything from creating a philosophy that members value to designing operational procedures that allow autonomy. According to Fred Smith, CEO of Federal Express, it is important to remember that employees' satisfaction is a prerequisite to customers' satisfaction (Reynolds 1992). For higher education institutions, it translates into training and educating employees so that they understand the significance of satisfying their numerous stakeholders.

In a survey of institutions with experience in implementing the quality principles, almost every respondent mentioned "involving people" and "giving them a voice" as key benefits of the quality movement (Seymour and Collett 1991). Organizations that excel in the future will be ones that "discover how to tap people's commitment and capacity to learn at all levels of the organization" (Senge 1990, p. 4). Once people are empowered, they need to be trained to collaborate so that they can effectively work in teams. Empowered teams are the building blocks of quality improvement.

Individual empowerment is epitomized in a poem by Lao Tsu in *Tao Te Ching:*

Organizations that excel in the future will be ones that "discover how to tap people's commitment and capacity to learn at all levels of the organization" (Senge 1990, p. 4).

> Go to the people.
> Learn from them.
> Love them.
> Start with what they know.
> Build on what they have.
> But of the best leaders,
> when their task is accomplished,
> their work is done, the people will remark:
> We have done it ourselves.

COLLABORATION

No one of us is as smart as all of us.

—Anonymous

There is no "I" in team.

—Anonymous

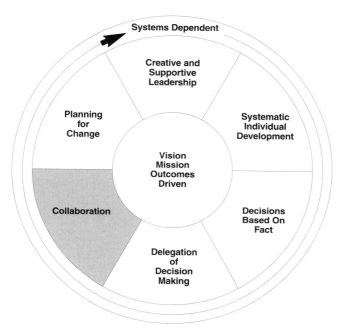

People who have a stake in the outcomes of a process have a vested interest in collaborating to improve the processes that create those outcomes. By 2000, an estimated 90 percent of all American companies will have their workforces structured as teams. As the quality principles are practiced in higher education institutions, collaboration and empowered work teams will be the trend. The complex and difficult problems facing higher education demand a new approach to solving problems that is based on bringing people together—those who are most influenced—to make decisions (Thor 1995).

While departments more often function as work teams, campus committees typically function as groups of individuals that get burdened with administrative tasks. The norm is that committees function politically, or they do not function at all (Ewell 1993). In contrast, collaboration involves learning new behaviors and changing the way people perceive their work. Quality improvement teams are created with authority and therefore empowered to address specific problems. Teams are action oriented; they study a particular problem with the goal to improve the system.

The task of forming teams is especially complicated for colleges and universities, because they are loosely coupled, open systems with multiple and poorly defined goals (Cohen and March 1984). They are decentralized, particularly in academic administration, but this decentralization is not necessarily synonymous with participatory processes (Winter 1991). "Industry desperately needs to foster teamwork. The only training or education on teamwork our people receive in school is on the athletic field. Teamwork in the classroom is called cheating" (W. Edwards Deming, cited in Gabor 1990, p. 25). Although collaboration and teamwork remains the means and not the end, improving work performance is the objective.

The concept of collaboration and teamwork in colleges and universities is complicated by several factors. Obstacles to teamwork include the tradition of academic freedom, the competitiveness of individual departments for funds and students, and a fundamental American individualism. Faculty members are accustomed to working independently, often competing with each other. The idea of working together to improve quality suggests a uniformity with which they are not comfortable. One of the major elements of higher education, the peer review for tenure, focuses on individual achievements, whereas the quality principles emphasize the achievements of teams. Traditionally, academic decision makers in colleges and universities act autonomously. Therefore, gaining acceptance for the idea of collaboration, particularly on the academic side, may be a challenge for any institution. For the quality principles to be successfully implemented in higher education, however, collaboration and teamwork must become the norm.

Implementing the concept of teams necessitates a shift for the culture of higher education. A team is a "small number of people with complementary skills who are committed to a common purpose, performance goals, and an approach for which they hold themselves mutually accountable" (Katzenbach and Smith 1993, p. 45). Based on research about higher education leadership teams, what a team is and what it is not can be clearly distinguished (Bensimon and Neumann 1993, p. 30). A team is not:

- A physical object that comes to life on the basis of clearly prescribed roles.
- A rational structure acting intentionally to achieve defined ends.
- A machine that can be analyzed purely in terms of its members' discrete behaviors.
- A tool that managers can use to further their ends.

In contrast, a team *is:*

- A collective unit that is an entity in and of itself, rather than merely the sum of its individual members.
- A set of actions, feelings, and experiences.
- A setting marked by both shared and fractured meaning.
- A social reality created and re-created by those who are part of it.
- A reality—complex and often inconsistent—that exists inside the head of each member and is perhaps different from member to member.
- A reality that is understood through close interpretation of the experiences of individual members.
- A fluid set of beliefs, understandings, and differences— sometimes consistent and complementary, other times inconsistent and contradictory—encompassing members and exceeding them even as they create and re-create meaning, conflict, and ambiguity (Bensimon and Neumann 1993).

As these differences indicate, a team is a process, not a product. The challenge for anyone who is responsible for building a team is to develop a group of people so that they are able to lead, act, and think together. The team should be able to think in more expansive and creative ways than any one person individually (Bensimon and Neumann 1993).

The disciplined application of "team basics" (size, purpose, goals, skills, approach, and accountability) is often overlooked in team processes (Katzenbach and Smith 1993). Teams are often perceived in an active state of doing and acting, but what is essential is *team thinking.* How team members perceive, discover, think, and create individually and interactively influences the team's success. Team processes are important in creating an effective team. The structure needs to involve building relationships that encourage connectedness, interaction, and collaboration. One way to do so is to encourage appropriate self-disclosure among peers (Bensimon and Neumann 1993). People need to feel comfortable with each other to build trusting relationships.

Quality might be initiated in the hearts and minds of senior leaders, but it lives in the work of teams. Better solutions emerge when everyone involved is allowed to collaborate to solve problems (Hillenmeyer 1992). In a culture embodying quality, situations are created in which teams, not individuals, have a whole and meaningful project to do. And the team has considerable autonomy in how it accomplishes the work (Lawler 1992). Moreover, the *team* receives feedback about the work. Collaboration and teamwork can be promoted in higher education by making it a stated goal of the institution and by senior leaders' endorsing the idea and supporting its implementation. It needs to become the way people think about accomplishing their work.

Collaboration and teamwork allow people to compensate for someone's weaknesses with someone else's strengths; the whole is greater than the sum of its parts. "Alignment" has been used to refer to a group of people functioning as a whole (Senge 1990), accomplished through a "commonality of purpose, a shared vision, and an understanding of how to complement one another's efforts" (p. 234). "Alignment is the necessary condition before empowering the individual will empower the whole team" (p. 235). When teams learn, they become a microcosm for learning throughout the organization (Senge 1990).

Using project teams, task forces, and committees to solve problems and make decisions in higher education is not new. But the idea of using teams trained together in decision making based on collecting and understanding data *is*. Teams are different from traditional committees, because members have been empowered to change the processes in which they work. Members assume different roles within the team to facilitate effective interaction. Senior leaders empower the teams, listen to the ideas presented, and make decisions based on the team's data and recommendations. Mechanisms to ensure continuous feedback from senior leaders increase the probability that the team's recommendations are feasible and realistic (Hillenmeyer 1992; Schmidt and Finnigan 1992).

Developing members to work effectively in teams involves educating them with a common knowledge and language about the process of improving quality. Specifically, members must be trained in meeting techniques, analysis, synthesis, team building, problem solving, and statistical tools. The important point is that collaboration and teamwork must be designed into the system; it involves more than *telling* people to work together (Hillenmeyer 1992).*

The training provided should:

- Teach employees how to communicate in a team, which involves understanding team dynamics and learning how to build a consensus.
- Teach team leaders how to organize team meetings that follow systematic agendas.
- Enhance team members' ability to analyze problems, evaluate alternatives, and plan and implement solutions using data in all phases of the analysis.
- Teach members tools that can be used in analyzing data.
- Encourage and reward cooperation and the sharing of information (Holpp 1989).

Teamwork involves meetings, and training in how to lead team meetings is necessary. These group experiences are important because they affect how people feel about their team, how committed they are to decisions, and how well they work as a team and individually. If meetings can be improved, teamwork, communications, morale, and productivity can be improved as well (Doyle and Straus 1976). To accomplish this goal, team members must have a clear definition of their roles:

- *Team leaders* plan meetings, distribute agendas in advance, and ensure that the team completes the plans for action.
- *Facilitators* make suggestions for solving problems, keep the team focused, and ensure that everyone has a chance to participate.

*The Team Handbook: How to Use Teams to Improve Quality (Scholtes 1988) and The Team Handbook for Educators: How to Use Teams to Improve Quality (Scholtes 1994) are common resources for building teams.

- *Team members* attend meetings, contribute ideas, collect data, recommend solutions, and help to implement them (Coate 1991).
- *Recorders,* who are neutral, nonevaluative servants of the group, create a "group memory" of everything that is said and display it so that the memory is visible for the whole group (Doyle and Straus 1976).

Successful organizations use the following 10 guiding questions to make meetings more effective and efficient (Schmidt and Finnigan 1992). Team leaders should ask these questions before calling a meeting of the team:

1. Why hold the meeting? The answer to this question—or the lack of one—will dictate the need for the meeting.
2. What is the expected outcome? This answer determines the focus of the meeting and acts as a benchmark for the actual outcome.
3. What type of meeting is it? Members should be informed as to whether the meeting is to solve problems, share information, gather data, or make decisions.
4. Based on the type of meeting planned, have the right people been included? The right people with the right information are essential.
5. Has sufficient time been allocated? Assign times for each part of the meeting plan and use the time accordingly.
6. Was an agenda distributed with enough lead time? Participants will be better prepared if the agenda, including start and stop times, a purpose, and desired outcomes, has been distributed far enough ahead of the meeting so they know what to expect.
7. How will the team deal with agenda items? Members need to understand group processes so they can act efficiently and productively.
8. Who does what? The various roles need to be decided and rotated among members.
9. How will decisions be made during the meeting? In a team, every opinion is valued, and teams usually reach a decision through consensus.
10. Who will make the final decision? Everyone should know.

Even the process of communicating in a team meeting is different from that for a typical committee meeting. The main difference is the one between a dialogue and a discussion. In a dialogue, members explore complex issues rather than trying to convince others of a particular viewpoint, and new actions emerge as a result of the dialogue. A dialogue develops trust that carries over to discussions. Because skills of building a consensus and working together to solve problems are difficult to learn, teams need to practice the various skills and evaluate the process at the end of each meeting so the process can continue to improve (Senge 1990).

"The viability of organizations as systems and their ability to meet expectations of external constituencies [depend] largely on whether and how internal interactions take place" (Ruben 1995b, p. 16). In a traditional bureaucratic setting, organizations have been structured around functions. In a manufacturing firm, for example, the typical functions are marketing, finance, production, sales, and human resources. In higher education, the functions are departments and divisions. Each function is organized hierarchically so that vertical structures or barriers (often described as walls, chimneys, or silos) are created that facilitate interaction *within* functional divisions. In other words, the structures become obstacles to interaction, coordination, and collaboration *between* functions. When this situation occurs, individuals and departments commonly lose sight of the institution's overall vision, mission, and outcomes. Work becomes departmentalized and an it's-not-my-job mentality emerges (Ruben 1995b). These barriers foster internal competition, a decreased sense of personal responsibility for achievement of the organization's mission, and a willingness to blame others outside the department instead of collaboration, cooperation, and teamwork.

When employees work in teams, they need to be able to cross departmental lines to gain an understanding of other units' goals, procedures, and practices. Cross-functional interactions reinforce the concept of systems thinking, and this holistic understanding of systems allows members to focus on the institution's common goals rather than on the department's goals (May 1991). The result is that everyone shares in the success of working together effectively.

If they do not function effectively, teams should revisit the *team basics* (Katzenbach and Smith 1993). Members should rethink the team's purpose, approach, and goals. Clarifying the team's mission and focusing on challenging performance goals is the best way to get back on target.

Teams do have disadvantages: They can become isolated and detached from the larger setting, and they can become victims of "groupthink" (Janis 1972), which means that the team fails to engage in critical thinking because it strives for consensus. In other words, the advantages of using teams to make decisions are lost when groupthink occurs. To minimize this possibility, the team could appoint a devil's advocate, break the team into subgroups, and then reconvene as a full group, or have the team leader take a nondirective role (Janis 1972). These strategies encourage members' full participation and help to prevent groupthink. The work involved in designing and nurturing effective teams is worth it, resulting in several advantages: creative problem solving among diverse individuals, peer support for one another, and increased accountability (Bensimon and Neumann 1993). In addition, teams help to develop a shared vision and ownership of the outcomes.

One national survey found team development to be the most important benefit of the quality movement because it addresses the most critical element of all the quality principles: the people within the institution (Seymour and Collett 1991). Likewise, data support the conclusion that redesigning the workplace around high-performance, self-directed teams yields significant gains in performance (Lawler 1986). Teams yield dramatically improved quality, decision making, work methods, employee retention, and safety. And effective leadership teams improve institutional performance and satisfaction (Bensimon and Neumann 1993). Therefore, teams that lead, act, and think together must replace the conventional idea of teams. According to Jamie Houghton, CEO of Corning, "If you really believe in quality, when you cut through everything, it's empowering your people, and it's empowering your people that leads to teams" (Dumaine 1990, p. 52).

The underlying factor affecting all the quality principles is the concept of change, which involves changing how decisions are made and who is accountable for making decisions, in turn requiring changed skills and knowledge through education and training. All of these changes depend on changing the behaviors of leaders so that they are able to empower others and build effective leadership teams. Creating a culture of excellence is based on making change a positive and continuous element of the institutional culture.

PLANNING FOR CHANGE

The only constant is change.

—Anonymous

The continued health of the operations of any organization depends on clever adaptation, alert changes, [and] daring innovations (Keller 1983, p. 167).

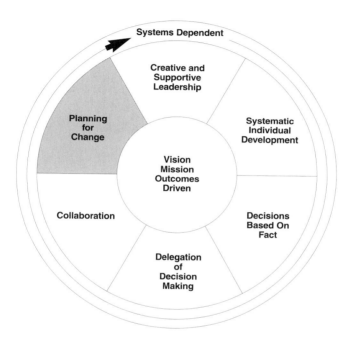

One of the major assumptions underlying the principle that a quality organization's vision, mission, and outcomes are driven by stakeholders' expectations is that stakeholders' expectations are continuously changing. Thus, the concept behind continuous improvement is the necessity for an organization to be alert to its stakeholders' continuously changing expectations and to the notion that planning for change must become an active and positive value in the culture. This principle does not refer to a planning process, but to a mind-set in each individual in the institution. It is an attitude about planning and an attitude about change. It involves embracing continuous change as an everyday element in the culture, an element to be cultivated, nurtured, and reinforced.

Everyone must change, but the change goes deeper than changing practices and techniques. Embracing change as a cultural value touches not what institutional members do, but who they are—not just their sense of the task, but their sense of themselves and not just what they know, but what they think (Champy 1995).

Higher education institutions, steeped in historical origins and precedence, are more likely than most organizations to have a culture that naturally resists change. With their long history of practices and traditions based on an accumulation of consistently acted-out values—for example, academic areas organized by department and based on disciplines or specialized areas of inquiry, presidents selected more for academic than administrative accomplishments, curricula determined by faculty with little or no external input, faculty assessed only by their peers—higher education institutions are often too entrenched to change easily and prefer the comfort of the status quo. The norm in higher education institutions is to measure success by the procedures—which tend to remain consistent over time with no evaluation of the current relevancy of the processes that operate within the procedures. In other words, the problem with these consistent traditions is that an institution is rarely viewed as a system and the relationships within the system are therefore often unexamined and disconnected.

The first of Deming's 14 points of management is *constancy of purpose,* where the intent is to relentlessly pursue a clearly articulated mission (1986). Deming did not mean that organizations should stay the same and never change. On the contrary, once an organization's purpose is clearly defined through its vision, mission, and outcomes, it is management's obligation to make whatever changes are necessary to achieve that purpose (p. 24). For example, if an institution's major goal or purpose is to have a highly diverse faculty and student body, then the excuse that applicant pools are not adequate would not be tolerated. With constancy of purpose, all recruiting processes would be evaluated and new processes tried until the purpose of having an institution with the appropriate mix of faculty and students is achieved.

Although higher education institutions are bound by tradition, history reveals that higher education institutions change constantly. Course offerings change, majors change, and stakeholders' expectations change. As stakeholders determine the mission and purpose of a nonprofit organization, it is expected that the mission should change to reflect stakeholders' needs and wants. Yet institutions are slow to change their missions, preferring to hold onto their traditions from the past. The result is tension between what the institution is doing and what stakeholders think it should be doing.

Institutions need to acknowledge the constant change in stakeholders' needs and expectations and make this pressure for change a conscious and positive part of the organization's culture. For example, a number of business and engineering schools have responded to their industrial stakeholders by teaching the quality principles because the industries need these skills and knowledge (Roberts 1995).

Change in higher education is inevitable and accelerating, and one need only look at the tremendous changes taking place as a result of communication via the Internet. Many academic areas, especially the health, science, and professional schools, are seeing new knowledge develop exponentially. For institutions to handle these new demands, they must perceive change as positive rather than be threatened by the call for change. Institutions need to create a culture that values change by developing a system that is able to stay in tune with the changes.

Institutions need to create a culture that values change by developing a system that is able to stay in tune with the changes.

CREATIVE AND SUPPORTIVE LEADERSHIP

Leadership involves moving others toward a shared perception of reality, toward a common understanding of where the organization is and where it should be going, and toward an increased commitment to those ends (Birnbaum 1992, p. 16).

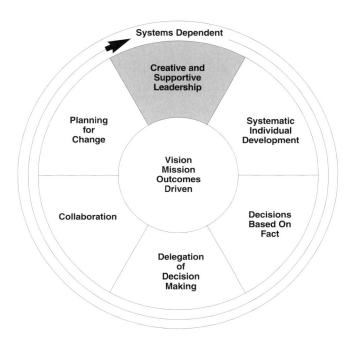

Shifting from an emphasis on resources to an emphasis on performance takes a new type of leader—one who is willing to take risks and involve other people. A leader is a person you follow to a place you would not go by yourself (Freed, Klugman, and Fife 1995). By involving and empowering others throughout the institution, members at all levels and in a variety of areas can take on leadership roles. The focus moves from controlling to influencing, a significant change because continuous improvement is based on continuous change. Being able to influence others to accept change as a cultural value and to influence members to implement change are essential characteristics in leaders.

Creating a quality culture requires leaders to demonstrate different skills and behaviors from those of the past (Ross 1993, p. 46). The new skills and behaviors are based on thinking differently about the institution and about how work should be done. Leaders' responsibilities in a quality culture include seeing that the institution's vision, mission, and outcomes are established and clearly understood (Beckhard and Prichard 1992, pp. 25–35; Covey 1991, p. 262). Leaders are the primary drivers of the quality initiatives on campus (Freed, Klugman, and Fife 1994; Thor 1996). The new role for leaders includes ensuring that the systems are in place so that the quality principles can be implemented. Moreover, it is important that people in positions of leadership provide the resources necessary to support the effort to instill quality if the quality principles are to be integrated into the institution's culture.

An underlying premise of the quality principles is that leadership is needed early during their implementation to create a quality culture and that strong leadership is important later in the process to support the change. Because the principles define a holistic approach to managing institutions, the principle of leadership brings the principles full circle, reinforcing the idea of a system.

> *Human beings are designed for learning. . . . Unfortunately, the primary institutions of our society are oriented predominately toward controlling rather than learning, rewarding individuals for performing for others rather than for cultivating their natural curiosity and impulse to learn* (Senge 1990, p. 7).

Leadership is the shared construction of meaning (Bensimon and Neumann 1993). "It requires uncovering the meaning that is already embedded in others' minds, helping them to see what they already know, believe, and value, and encouraging them to make new meaning. In this way leadership generates leadership" (p. xv). Moreover, "leadership is not a zero-sum game, but a process of reciprocal influence in which power increases as it is shared. Good leaders beget more good leaders" (Birnbaum 1992, p. 122).

Most organizations are underled and overmanaged (Birnbaum 1992; Nanus 1992). Employees tend to be programmed to do what they are told; they are not focused on thinking for themselves (Lawler 1992). "Our prevailing system of management has destroyed our people" (W. Edwards Deming, cited in Senge 1990, p. 7), and 94 percent of the problems in organizations are the result of poor management or are at least the responsibility of leadership (Deming 1986).

Because the quality movement is based on changing institutional systems, a new type of leadership is required.

> *Managers want to deny that people have problems and fears. They walk around with blinders, trying to attend to their "managerial duties." They are able to keep their distance from workers because of the absorbing layers of middle [managers], whose job is to keep a lid on problems. What these managers are ignoring is that their job is dealing with employees' problems, eliminating their fears, and encouraging the development of people* (Gitlow and Gitlow 1987, p. 137).

For organizations to break with the stereotypical management practices of the past, managers must take the lead. "Leadership is the thread that weaves the other 13 Deming points together and forms the basis for a tapestry of concepts that could improve the leadership and management of postsecondary education" (Hyson 1991, p. 72). Although leaders need employees to cooperate, it is leaders' responsibility to begin the change. It is also their responsibility to support the system, making sure that the other systems are in place to reinforce the quality culture (Ryan and Oestreich 1991; Thomson and Roberts 1992).

How leaders spend their time, where they spend it, and how they communicate (writing and speaking) lead to different understandings about how members within an institution can influence leadership and decision making. Creating cultural symbols and helping people determine the meaning of symbols are also important responsibilities for leaders (Kuh and Whitt 1988). The success of instituting the quality principles depends on the effectiveness of leaders.

The effectiveness of colleges and universities depends to a great degree on the effectiveness of administrators (Whetten and Cameron 1985). Research on administrative effectiveness in higher education revealed eight principles that substantiate many of the quality principles:

1. *Place equal emphasis on process and outcomes.* Effective administrators are concerned about the process of implementing a decision (the systems of the organization)

as well as the content of the decision (the outcomes). In a time of declining resources, they are described as fair, open to dialogue, and trustworthy. This principle reflects characteristics needed to lead the movement toward quality.

2. *Do not be afraid of failure; be willing to take risks.* Effective leaders keep focused on long-term outcomes while building systems that will minimize the chance of failure. These systems allow members the freedom to take risks by providing a supportive environment. A quality culture should drive out fear and empower members to take the initiative.

3. *Nurture the support of strategic constituencies.* Effective administrators build a successful coalition by continually cultivating political and financial support. They understand that developing these relationships is vital during periods of decline and organizational success. A systems orientation means that stakeholders' expectations are part of the system that needs to be monitored, nurtured, and translated into the institution's mission and outcomes.

4. *Do not succumb to the numerous demands of interest groups.* Effective administrators are able to distinguish between legitimate needs that further the organization's mission and strongly advocated needs that more often further more personal objectives. By articulating a clear vision and institutional mission, a quality leader is able to prioritize demands and stay focused.

5. *Leave a distinctive imprint.* Administrators found to be effective left a legacy because they were able to assess the institution's strengths and weaknesses, opportunities for it, and threats to it while caring about the faculty's morale and students' concerns. A quality leader always considers stakeholders' expectations and creates an empowering culture in which they can participate.

6. *Err in favor of overcommunication, especially during times of flux.* Information reduces uncertainty; thus, the more information people have, the less fearful they will be about uncertainty. When enrollments are declining, funding is being reduced, and changes to curricula or personnel are being proposed, the need is greater for administrators to communicate information about priorities, constraints, and changes. Effective communication

is essential to empower others, build teams based on trust, and create a culture that supports quality.

7. *Respect the power of institutional culture.* Effective administrators respect the indigenous institutional culture. When they demonstrate an awareness of and sensitivity to the shared values already in existence, they are able to win members' trust and confidence. This allegiance must take place before any major changes can occur. Although the quality principles are a change in culture, the core values and norms are aligned with the institution's mission and outcomes. This culture is possible when fear is driven out of the institution and replaced by the leaders' trust and confidence.

8. *Preserve and highlight institutional sources of opportunity at any cost.* Effective administrators are able to convert crises into mandates for improvement. They shift the faculty's attention away from visible signs of financial crises by stimulating enthusiasm for new opportunities. They maintain an offensive position. Similarly, the quality movement is based on continuous improvement of all systems. Continuous change is perceived as a positive element of the culture, and searching for opportunities to improve is of the highest priority (Whetten and Cameron 1985).

Findings of the Institutional Leadership Project (Birnbaum 1992) identify characteristics of successful presidents that reflect the quality leadership advocated in this monograph. Presidents were classified into one of three categories: modal, failed, and exemplary. Modal presidents had an average presidency that began with high support from all constituencies but ended with support from the trustees and administrators only, not from faculty or students. Failed presidents began like modal presidents but ended with the president's losing the confidence of all constituencies, starting with students and faculty and eventually the administration and the board. The loss of confidence was the result of an inability to handle criticism. The response of the failed president was to discount, ignore, reject, and finally withdraw from groups that criticized the president. By doing so, the president did not solve any disagreements and finally lost the support of the groups.

In contrast, exemplary presidents were able to maintain the support of faculty, trustees, and administrators throughout their tenure. Exemplary presidents demonstrated quality leadership by continuing to cultivate faculty support during the entire presidency. They were enthusiastic, committed to the institution, and sought interaction with faculty like a new president. They were recognized for making effective decisions and for following systematic processes. Exemplary presidents perceived faculty as the institution's strength; they therefore developed a collaborative relationship with them. Through constant interaction with all the institution's constituencies, the exemplary president was able to create a shared vision. One exemplary president expressed his perception of leadership thus:

> *By sharing influence, I have greatly influenced my own influence. They know I'm willing to listen, so they listen to me. I think the college is a political system. The president can't force others to do something, only persuade* (Birnbaum 1992, p. 101).

Managers and leaders in higher education are people in administrative positions. Often the misperception exists that "managers" and "leaders" are synonymous, but effective administrators are leaders rather than managers. Management is often defined as an activity that keeps an organization running and works well in an organized hierarchy. Leadership, on the other hand, involves getting things started and facilitating change (Huey 1994). As organizations have decreased the number of administrators and flattened out organizational charts, the emphasis has shifted from managing to leading. The new role calls for leaders to "create change and set the direction in which the organization moves, thereby controlling the change rather than allowing the organization to be controlled by the change. This type of leadership requires significant paradigm shifts" (Thor 1995, p. 4).

In an increasingly dynamic, interdependent, and challenging environment, it is no longer possible for people at the top of the organization to have all the answers. The new leadership is responsible for building organizations in which people at all levels continually learn through being involved in making decisions. Many organizations are "recognizing that empowerment and autonomy can help them respond effectively to rapid changes in the business environment" (Carr 1994, p. 39). A commitment to the quality principles usually involves a change in management style (Freed, Klugman, and Fife 1994); 63 percent of respondents noted that their institutions had a more collegial style of leadership after implementing the principles. On a scale of 1 (indicating autocratic) to 7 (indicating collegial), the mean management score before implementing the quality principles was 3.2 and after implementation was 4.1.

Interestingly, leadership training has not typically been a part of professional development for many administrators. Administrators often arrive in managerial positions from a variety of disciplines and must learn a new way of thinking and behaving in their new roles. "Rarely does the status quo change without people in leadership positions having the knowledge of self and the repertoire of skills that allow them to behave differently" (Leffel et al. 1991, p. 64). For administrators to behave differently, institutions must provide leaders with the skills and knowledge they need to break traditional patterns.

Although the experts agree that leadership is critical, Deming (1986) strongly emphasizes the importance of an empowering rather than controlling leadership. Deming describes leaders as coaches who counsel, not judge, and emphasizes cooperation, not competition. The leadership of the future is based on building relationships, trust, and letting go (Wheatley 1994).

The key to leadership exists in creating a shared vision and making clear the distinction between enrollment, commitment, and compliance (Senge 1990). To buy into the institutional vision communicates the idea of selling—getting people to do things they might not otherwise do. Enrolling means choosing to become part of something. Committed people feel willing to participate; in contrast, compliance implies acting out of obligation. Relatively few people enroll in organizations, and even fewer are committed to them. Most are in a state of compliance in which they go with the flow and do only what is expected of them.

For people to want to enroll in efforts to improve quality, leaders must model the desired behaviors. Employees need to be given freedom of choice and not feel pressured into compliance. Enrolling must be a personal decision if commitment is to be the outcome. A committed person brings energy, excitement, and passion to the workplace because of a belief in the vision and a sense of responsibility for working toward the objective. The only way for a leader to evoke commitment in others is to be committed. Figure 22 illustrates Senge's commitment ladder; it distinguishes compliance from commitment and describes varying degrees of buying-in associated with points along a continuum ranging from noncompliance to commitment.

FIGURE 22

The Commitment Ladder

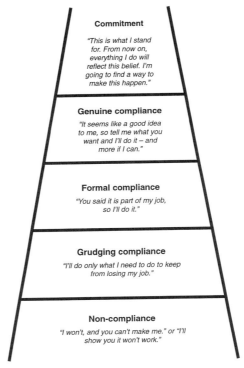

Commitment

"This is what I stand for. From now on, everything I do will reflect this belief. I'm going to find a way to make this happen."

Genuine compliance

"It seems like a good idea to me, so tell me what you want and I'll do it – and more if I can."

Formal compliance

"You said it is part of my job, so I'll do it."

Grudging compliance

"I'll do only what I need to do to keep from losing my job."

Non-compliance

"I won't, and you can't make me." or "I'll show you it won't work."

Source: Thomson and Roberts 1992, p. 47.

In the educational context, an empowering leader creates an environment where innovation is encouraged, where faculty, staff, and administrators can take risks to improve processes within certain boundaries. To do so requires flexibility in adapting to various situations and changing conditions. An empowering leader encourages the faculty to provide superior educational experiences and encourages the staff to provide exceptional support services for students. This type of leadership requires people who are committed to listening, trusting, and respecting each person in the institution. "Everybody goes to work to do a good job, but stuff gets in the way. . . . It's up to the leader to get this stuff out of the way" (Baker 1994, p. 65).

Systems and processes will be improved if leaders focus on helping employees do their jobs successfully (Hyson 1991). The job of quality leaders is to make employees successful, and successful employees in turn will satisfy stakeholders' expectations (Crosby 1979). As a result, the organization will be successful.

Many high-ranking administrators are not necessarily effective quality leaders. Quality leadership requires different roles, among them teacher/coach and steward.

- *Leader as teacher and coach.* Leaders need to help others to lead themselves. As teachers, facilitators, and coaches, they should act as role models. Their behaviors should reflect the values and beliefs that are central to the organization. In addition, their behaviors need to be consistent and persistent, and they need to take a personal interest in the activities that improve processes and relationships with stakeholders. And leaders need to "talk the talk" but, more important, "walk the talk" (Leffel et al. 1991; LeTarte 1993; Peters 1987; Schmidt and Finnigan 1992). Instead of monitoring and controlling the behaviors of others, leaders teach and coach by encouraging others to learn, take risks, and become more involved.
- *Leader as steward.* Individuals who are stewards seek responsibility over entitlement and are accountable to those over whom they exercise power. When employees are allowed the authority to manage themselves, it is no longer necessary to pay a "watchdog." A "servant leader" is one who articulates goals, knows how to listen, inspires trust, and emphasizes personal development (Lee and Zemke 1993). Stewardship replaces self-interest; dependency, and control with service, responsibility, and partnerships (Block 1993; Greenleaf 1977; Senge 1990). Quality leaders also need to learn new skills:
- *Building a shared vision.* Leaders need to articulate a vision into which people want to enroll and be commit-

ted. The vision acts as a focus and provides a common bond for institutional members: "The rowers must row together" (Kiefer and Senge 1986). Synergy is created when everyone recognizes how much more can be accomplished collectively. The process of building a shared vision is a continual process. "The vision lives in the intensity of the leader, an intensity that in itself draws in others" (Peters 1987, p. 493).

- *Communication and feedback.* Leaders need to communicate the institution's mission as clearly and in as many ways as possible. If employees are to act in ways that support organizational effectiveness, they must understand the organization's mission, how the organization measures performance, what they can do to contribute to the mission, and how they can improve their performance. Leaders should explain how each strategic decision fits with the mission (Bass 1985; Burns 1978; Lawler 1992; Tichy and Devanna 1986). In return, leaders need to listen to employees and use this feedback to improve systems and make better decisions.

- *Listening.* "You can convey no greater honor than to actually hear what someone has to say" (Crosby 1979, p. 133). Shared visions can evolve from listening to employees' goals and dreams. The leader's role is to listen to what the organization is saying and then make sure it is articulated forcefully (Senge 1990). Exemplary college presidents listen intently to faculty (Birnbaum 1992). They are perceived as continuing to respond to the faculty's needs, and they support faculty governance. Successful presidents consider interaction with faculty to be rewarding and helpful, but it cannot happen without effective listening.

  To be able to listen effectively, certain mechanisms need to be integrated into the culture, including formal and informal opportunities for discussion among stakeholders. For colleges and universities, such opportunities include exit interviews with professors, administrators, and staff people to determine why they accepted other positions or with students who transferred to another institution.

- *A systems orientation.* Leaders need to develop a framework for understanding relationships within the institution rather than seeing separate parts. "Systems oriented" means viewing everyone as active participants in a sys-

tem. "Everyone shares responsibility for problems generated by a system" (Senge 1990, p. 78), and everyone can
therefore contribute to solving systemic problems. Table 6
illustrates the contrasts between the new model of quality
leadership and the old, traditional style of leadership.

TABLE 6

Two Models of Leadership

Characteristics	Quality Cultural Leadership	Traditional Leadership
Underlying Principles	**New Paradigm**	**Old Paradigm**
Values	Community/common good Collaboration Process/meaning making	Individualism/self-interest Expertise Task
Relationships	Egalitarian Followers share accountability Involvement with group members Recognizes multiple perspectives Relationship end in itself Power with	Hierarchical Followers are subservient Governed by Subordinate/ superordinate positions Recognizes one view Relationship means to end Power over
Power	Empower members Share power Create meaning Rituals, symbols, ceremonies Staff autonomy All members accessible Shared voice in decision-making Legitimacy based on confidence from informal network (group)	Control members Wield power Manage resources Personnel, financial, etc. Jobs delineated, well definable Leaders inaccessible Little or no voice in decision-making Legitimacy of position

Communication	Allows for making meaning across
	   channels
	All members have voice
	Inclusive network of relationship
	
	Empower
	Persuasion
	Conflict is mediated/negotiated
	Listen in order to understand others
	   context
	Win-win
	Accessible to followers
		Control - top down
		
		Those with power have voice
		Exclusive relationships as means to
		   further ends
		Decisive
		Coercion
		Conflict determined by leader
		Going through motions of listening for
		   political reasons
		Win-lose
		Separate from followers

Source: Adapted from Guido-DiBrito and Nathan 1995.

These new roles and skills are vital if leaders are to provide
new answers to the same old questions. Although the old
answer, top-down control, might have been strong, the new
answer is local control united by purpose or vision. The old

approach focused on the operating unit; the new one focuses on the entire system. Cooperation and teamwork replace competition. The norm has shifted from trying to avoid change to anticipating and addressing change. Channels of communication must be open to allow information to flow more freely (Thor 1995). As facilitators and coaches, "leaders are successful not when they act, but when they enable others to act" (Carr 1994, p. 44). Only when employees can say "we did it ourselves" will leaders know that they have truly led.

A survey of 15,000 people identified characteristics of effective leaders (Kouzes and Posner 1993). The top four characteristics and the percentage of people who selected them were honest (87 percent), forward looking (71 percent), inspirational (68 percent), and competent (58 percent). The researchers concluded that honest people have credibility that fosters trust and confidence in others. Credible leaders do what they say they will do by following through on commitments. Their actions are consistent with what others value, and they believe in the value of others. They are able to communicate the shared values and visions that form a common ground. They are capable of developing leaders around them by admitting their mistakes, diminishing fear in others. Credible leaders are optimistic and give others hope about the possibilities of success. And they create a climate for learning characterized by trust and openness (Kouzes and Posner 1993). In essence, credible leaders are quality leaders. They adhere to the quality principles.

"Leadership is always dependent on the context but the context is established by the relationships we value. We cannot hope to influence any situation without respect for the complex network of people who contribute to our organizations" (Wheatley 1994, p. 144). Changing the culture is a gradual process. What leaders do to articulate and act on their visions must be congruent with the history and traditions of the institution's cultural context (Kuh and Whitt 1988). Top administrators need to demonstrate respect for all employees and for the existing culture, realizing that everyone is part of an interdependent system.

The quality principles will not be effective in the absence of committed leaders at the top of the institution (Sashkin and Kiser 1993; Thomson and Roberts 1992), and "leaders are successful only when they empower others to help create and share the mission, to trust one another, to coordinate and communicate with one another, and to create and learn together" (Carr 1994, p. 44).

Capable leaders are essential to thinking as a team. If teams are to be effective, leaders must pay attention to team processes that are often overlooked. They must be strongly committed to following through on team processes, which usually requires unlearning traditional traits of leadership—aggressiveness, competitiveness, and authoritarianism. In a quality culture, leadership is redefined as collective, shared, interactive, and engaged if teams are to lead, act, and think effectively together. A study of presidential leadership teams identified two characteristics of presidents who consistently foster an atmosphere of openness in their leadership teams: (1) They are sensitive to and appreciate interpersonal processes, and (2) they have a good understanding of themselves (Bensimon and Neumann 1993, p. 108). Moreover, they are open, leading to a team environment based on trust.

A series of focus group interviews with academic leaders from deans to presidents identified five areas in which academic leaders should channel their efforts:

In a quality culture, leadership is redefined as collective, shared, interactive, and engaged...

1. *Emphasizing the concept of quality, not language.* Business and management terms are not well received in the academic community. Changing to more culturally sensitive language helps to avoid conflicts over rhetoric.
2. *Making faculty members aware of their institutional responsibilities.* Faculty will admit that the administrative side of the academy can benefit from the quality principles, but they are reluctant to believe that the academic side can benefit as well. Faculty must be convinced that the quality principles could increase students' learning.
3. *Breaking down barriers among organizational units.* Faculty have a great deal of autonomy, which can lead to isolation. They tend to work alone, viewing themselves as independent contractors rather than members of an institution and aligning themselves with their disciplines instead of the institution where they are employed. Collaboration and teamwork can be used in any department trying to improve systems processes, and leaders should set the example by including faculty members on process improvement teams.
4. *Restructuring reward systems.* Collaboration should be rewarded, which is generally not the case. Leaders must

be willing to engage the institution in rethinking its fundamental values and rewards. This component is important in changing behaviors.

5. *Building trust so that assumptions can be challenged.* Colleges and universities are structured to resist change, and people are attracted to the academy who are comfortable with a sense of history, traditions, and lack of change. Leaders have to continually articulate the idea that change is positive (Dhiman and Seymour 1996).

Leaders are responsible for defining reality as an environment in which change can and must evolve to everyone's credit (Dhiman and Seymour 1996).

It is leaders' role to create a culture where everyone within the institution is trained in leadership, treated like leaders, and expected to lead. In a quality culture, all members' leadership abilities are optimized and used (Batten 1994). After they do, however, leaders must strive to provide the resources necessary to support the improvement of quality on campus. Creating a culture for academic excellence is a gradual, but continual, process. It is leaders' responsibility to ensure that the resources are available to support the implementation of the quality principles.

THE IMPLICATIONS OF IMPLEMENTING
THE QUALITY PRINCIPLES

*We're not there yet, and we probably never will be, but
we keep trying to do better* (Schmidt and Finnigan 1992,
p. 343).

Even though it is hard to define, who can be against quality?
The quality principles are effective management practices
that result in a new management philosophy. The quality
movement is based on a different set of assumptions, a new
paradigm for management:

- Be aware of whom you serve and how best to satisfy
  their needs.
- Every position is part of a systemic process that affects
  and is affected by other positions.
- Individuals must be trained in structured problem solving,
  which includes knowledge of how to conduct a meeting.
- Decisions must be based on facts.
- The people who know the work best are the ones who
  perform it.
- Groups of people collaborating in teams can often have
  more success than individuals working alone if they have
  a stake in the outcomes (Walton 1990).

Interestingly, colleges with high faculty morale have similar
characteristics: empowering leaders with a strong participatory style; a willingness to share information across the institution; collaboration and focused support, not competition;
and an intentionally flat, horizontal organizational structure
that minimizes hierarchial distinctions (Rice and Austin 1988).

The quality principles involve introducing new systems
and processes that result in better quality (see figure 23).
Better quality brings more pride in workmanship, resulting
in a change of attitudes and behaviors. New behaviors become a change in the culture, where the culture insists on
better systems and processes, which in turn produces improved results. The cycle results in continuous improvement
(Cornesky et al. 1992).

Implementing the quality principles in higher education
results in asking questions that are different from the traditional management questions. Figure 24 outlines specific
questions that should be asked and answered if the quality
principles are to make meaningful contributions to higher
education institutions (Ruben 1995a). The questions help to

---

translate the quality principles into action steps to be taken to improve processes and systems.

FIGURE 23

The Process for Introducing Change to Quality

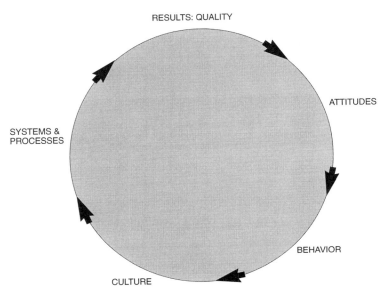

Source: Cornesky et al. 1992, p. 35.

A great deal of learning takes place along institutions' journey toward quality. Continuous improvement is about taking risks, learning from mistakes, and making changes for improvement. While none of it is hard to understand, none of it is easy to do (Walton 1990); therefore, several mistakes are common in the implementation of continuous improvement.

First, the organization's top management often lacks a commitment to the movement. If senior administrators remain uncommitted, the movement lacks the visionary leadership needed to facilitate and model the necessary cultural change. Committed leaders are necessary to build a culture that promotes educational quality. And committed leaders will work to continuously improve the culture.

Second, employees' support may be insufficient. Institutional change takes time, energy, and a long-term commitment from all those involved. Leaders must shift from managing to leading, from directing employees to empowering them. Employees must be open to change and be willing to take the responsibilities asked of them.

FIGURE 24

The Quality Assessment and Improvement Process

1. Development, refinement, and/or review of the institution's/unit's mission, vision, and goals.

   - Why does the institution/unit exist?
   - What services do we provide?
   - What products do we create?
   - How do we fit with and contribute to the overall mission of the institution and/or the unit in which we are located?
   - What goals and/or values guide our activities?
   - How would we ideally like to be seen?
   - To what extent do faculty and staff share a common understanding of our institution's/unit's mission, vision, and goals?

2. Identification of key consumer groups for each of the academic and service components of the institution/unit, and assessment of their needs and expectations.

   - For whom do we provide services and/or products (for instance, students, faculty, staff, alumni, potential employers, boards, taxpayers, funding sources, donors)?
   - Are there other constituency groups upon whose judgment we depend (for example, colleagues at other institutions, accreditation and regulatory bodies)?
   - What does each of these external constituency groups expect from us? How do we know?
   - What criteria do they use in assessing the services and/or products we provide?

3. Assessment of current levels of performance in each mission/vision/goal area.

   - How well does our unit do?
   - How do we assess our performance? What criteria do we use?
   - What are our strengths? Our weaknesses? Our limitations?
   - How do consumers for our services and/or products assess our performance?
   - What are the major courses of satisfaction and dissatisfaction with our services or products?
   - How does our performance compare to that at peer institutions? To other types of institutions?

4. Identification, analysis, and prioritization of gaps between: (a) mission/vision and current performance levels; (b) mission/vision and consumer expectations/satisfaction levels; and/or (c) consumer expectations and current performance levels.

   - What gaps exist between our performance and our vision of what we would like to be?
   - What gaps exist between our performance and the expectations of key constituency groups?
   - What gaps exist between our vision and expectations of key constituencies?
   - Which of these gaps have the greatest impact on key constituencies?
   - Which gaps are the result of performance problems?
   - Which gaps are a consequence of communication problems? Both?

5. Development of improvement strategies for eliminating or reducing selected gaps.

   - What options are available for reducing critical gaps?
   - What are the barriers and facilitators for each possibility?
   - What resources are required? (time, dollars, expertise)
   - What should the plan of action be? (How does it fit with and contribute to the overall mission of the unit and university?)
   - How will we know if the effort is successful?

6. Integration of changes into normal work processes.

   - What can be done to ensure continuation of the improvements (short term and long term)?
   - How can the changes be integrated into an improved work flow?
   - What needs to be done to ensure regular evaluation and improvement?

Source: Ruben 1995a, p. 170.

Third, institutions are reluctant to pay the costs associated with continuous improvement. But institutions must be willing to foot the bills for the costs of developing, educating, and reeducating administrators, faculty, and staff. The quality movement will not be an institutional priority without a strong commitment to covering its costs.

Fourth, higher education institutions are often not committed for the long term. Leaders need to prepare all participants to understand that the quality principles are a long-range philosophy and not a passing fad. In doing so, it is helpful to celebrate the small successes that build credibility for the quality movement (Wolverton 1993).

Fifth, the academic side of the institution is often not involved from the start. If faculty are not included when the quality movement is initiated, they perceive it to be an administrative approach rather than an operating philosophy affecting the entire institution (Freed, Klugman, and Fife 1994). Because the essence of education is teaching and learning, faculty must recognize that they too have an important part to play in improving the environment for a continually changing student body.

The lessons learned from practitioners in 25 institutions reinforce the quality principles presented in this report. Based on practical experience in implementing the quality principles in higher education institutions, practitioners had the following advice:

- Ensure committed leadership, for leadership is a critical factor.
- Train facilitators; they are essential.
- Demand an initial commitment from the board, president, and deans.
- Engage faculty in an intellectual dialogue about quality early in the process.
- Communicate the mission and vision statements to gain more understanding and ownership of the process.
- Resist jargon.
- Do not view continuous quality improvement as an end but a means for achieving desired outcomes and a tool for change.
- Clarify all employees' expectations about their role in contributing to continuous improvement.

- Change reward and incentive systems to encourage improvement in quality.
- Change performance appraisals, job descriptions, and recognition to incorporate the goals for quality.
- Spend time talking about organizational and cultural change to prepare employees for the transformation.
- Make training a top priority and allocate resources to support ongoing training.
- Integrate the quality movement with strategic planning.
- Emphasize personal change earlier by helping people understand that quality is a personal philosophy (American Association 1994).

The quality principles are consistent with the higher education environment (Chaffee and Seymour 1991). The principles are based on fundamental educational values, such as human resource development, life-long learning, rational problem solving, and societal benefit. But the quality principles are more than tools and techniques; they are a new institutional operating philosophy. The principles insist that the information students learn in the classroom be reinforced in the manner the university is being operated. "If the administrative and the academic processes can be in alignment with the mission, then the learning environment will be enhanced in ways that more effectively prepare students for the challenges of life" (Hull 1992, p. 238).

A conceptual shift in the movement from person-focused thinking to system-focused thinking is essential. Once this concept is understood, everything starts to change. Quality systems should be the basis for how work is performed, how people are held accountable, how people are evaluated, promoted, or disciplined, and how effectively services are provided. The concept of stakeholders or customers is still problematic, however. "If we can manage our institutions with the customers in mind, we will have come a long way to redefining higher education" (Seymour and Collett 1991, p. 25).

Based on experience implementing the quality principles, one college president observed:

The quality movement is still in process. Within the next several years our perceptions will change significantly as new learning is applied. The fact that one day we will be rethinking old ideas in light of new understanding should not cause us concern; instead of apologizing for having to shift gears, we will be aware that personal growth and learning are taking place (LeTarte 1993, p. 21).

That awareness is the reward for implementing the quality principles. Although the benefits of the effort to implement quality are not always quantifiable, some positive results are commonly cited. People actively engaged in the quality movement in higher education say that the quality movement can achieve efficiencies, raise morale, show good stewardship of funds, and win public trust—"time has been saved, costs have been reduced, people have been empowered at all levels, and morale has risen" (Coate 1990, p. 35)—but in the short term it is hard to measure cost savings (Marchese 1993).

Improved communication and improved customer satisfaction were two key benefits cited by approximately 65 percent of the respondents in one survey (Freed, Klugman, and Fife 1994). Approximately 50 percent of the respondents cited improved coordination and increased morale; approximately 30 percent indicated less rework and a changed culture. The study also discovered that the major frustration with the quality movement was the perception that it is a fad (63 percent), followed by the fact that implementation of the quality principles is time-consuming (62 percent) (see also Seymour 1992 and Seymour and Collett 1991).

The time involved and the support needed from senior leaders were frequently mentioned frustrations of implementing the quality principles (Freed, Klugman, and Fife 1994). Even so, the majority of respondents indicated that the benefits outweigh the costs and frustrations. Although they would have done some things differently, the consensus was that they would do it again. "Just get started" they said repeatedly, supporting the notion that "there is no right way" and the important decision is to begin the quality journey and to learn in the process.

"In our classrooms we encourage students to examine competing theories, test assumptions, create learning situations, and use critical thinking skills. Perhaps this is the time to apply what we teach to what we do" (Seymour and Collett 1991, p. 28). Quality is not a task to be added to people's lists of jobs. It should be an "everyday way of doing business" (Wolverton 1993, p. 2). The principles are not new or unique; what is new is the recognition that institutions must make a systematically conscious pursuit of quality, committed to all the principles simultaneously. Doing so may require a revolution in thinking and an evolution in practice, a dramatic change in the culture. It is difficult to unlearn behaviors that were successful in the past and traditionally reinforced through rewards; therefore, transforming higher education institutions with the quality principles will not be easy, nor will the process be expedient. The principles cannot be adopted piecemeal: The quality movement will be successful only if the principles are implemented simultaneously, adapted for each particular institution and improved over time.

Linear thinking still dominates most mental models used for critical decisions, but quality organizations make decisions based on shared understandings of relationships and patterns of change (Senge 1990). The principles require a disciplined approach that takes time and dedication.

The quality principles also involve a personal commitment to changing the mental model, which in turn transforms the culture of the institution. We must "commit ourselves to operate in a way that we believe in because it is what we have to do. . . . To live out a way of operating that we alone believe in gives real meaning to our work and to our lives" (Block 1989, pp. 194–95). Meaningful and lasting change starts on the inside and works its way out. Therefore, change cannot be imposed from the outside and expect it to be welcomed or to last (Tice 1993).

Ultimately, the quality movement is all about *people*. It is discovering how to learn, to grow, and to continue to improve personally and, by extension, institutionally. In education, quality is also about improving for the lives of those touched in the teaching process (Bonstingl 1993). Because quality is personal, it is everyone's responsibility. To make this point, Deming always concluded his seminars with the same five words: "I have done my best" (Walton 1986).

An analogy that embodies several of the quality principles is a flock of geese on the wing. Their system of flying in a "V" formation represents individuals who are aligned toward a common goal and share a common direction and sense of community. The lead goose breaks the airflow, making it easier for the other geese to follow because they are traveling on one another's thrust. When the lead goose tires, another goose takes its place, so the other geese must adjust to the continually changing leaders to accomplish the task at hand. More important, each goose is responsible for its own performance on the team. The geese fly in a wedge, but they land in waves (Graham and LeBaron 1994).

In summary, people should put aside their old ways of thinking (the old culture), learn to be open with others (quality leadership and the delegation of decision making), understand how their company (or institution) really works (a focus on systems), form a plan that everyone can agree upon (vision, mission, and outcomes driven), and then work together to achieve that vision (collaborate) (Peter Senge, cited in Dumaine 1994).

Northwest Missouri State University is an institution that early on decided to embrace the quality principles under the leadership of a president who champions quality.

> *At Northwest, we have kept our eyes on what we call a "culture of quality" for a long time. Achieving such a culture has been a driving force in our planning and development . . . for nearly a decade. We believe that such an environment provides the impetus for change, the support for risk taking, the commitment to continuous improvement. This culture is the culture for quality* (VanDyke 1995, p. xi).

President Ronald Reagan summarized the quality principles at the first ceremony honoring winners of the Malcolm Baldrige National Quality Award:

> *The one trait that characterizes these winners is that they realize that quality improvement is a never-ending process, a companywide effort in which every worker plays a critical part. . . . These awards are won by companies, but they are earned by individuals working together in the quest for excellence* (Ebel 1991, p. 12).

Continual success depends on being better tomorrow than today, and it is the basis for continuous improvement. The quality principles will not give us all the answers, but they force us to ask the right questions. And the questions being asked about quality improvement reflect a change in thinking about work and about institutions.

The quality principles are neither a panacea nor easy to implement. They require time, patience, and determination, but the institutions that have begun the journey believe the effort is worth it (American Association 1994, Freed and Klugman 1996). What kind of commitment does it take to systematically practice the quality principles and how long should it last? Deming's response to that question was "forever" (Sashkin and Kiser 1993).

REFERENCES

The Educational Resources Information Center (ERIC) Clearing-house on Higher Education abstracts and indexes the current literature on higher education for inclusion in ERIC's database and announcement in ERIC's monthly bibliographic journal, *Resources in Education* (RIE). Most of these publications are available through the ERIC Document Reproduction Service (EDRS). For publications cited in this bibliography that are available from EDRS, ordering number and price code are included. Readers who wish to order a publication should write to the ERIC Document Reproduction Service, 3900 Wheeler Avenue, Alexandria, Virginia 22304. (Phone orders with VISA or MasterCard are taken at 800/227-ERIC or 703/823-0500.) When ordering, please specify the document (ED) number. Documents are available as noted in microfiche (MF) and paper copy (PC). If you have the price code ready when you call, EDRS can quote an exact price. The last page of the latest issue of *Resources in Education* also has the current cost, listed by code.

Ackoff, Russell L. 1974. *Redesigning the Future: A Systems Approach to Societal Problems.* New York: Wiley.

————. 1995. "The Challenges of Change and the Need for Systems Thinking." Paper presented at the AAHE Conference on Assessment and Quality, June 11–14, Boston, Massachusetts.

Aguayo, Rafael. 1990. *Dr. Deming: The American Who Taught the Japanese about Quality.* New York: Carol Publishing Group.

American Association for Higher Education. 1994. *25 Snapshots of a Movement: Profiles of Campuses Implementing CQI.* Washington, D.C.: Author.

Anderson, M. 1992. *Impostors in the Temple: American Intellectuals Are Destroying Our Universities and Cheating Our Children of Their Future.* New York: Simon & Schuster.

Angelo, Thomas A., and K. Patricia Cross. 1993. *Classroom Assessment Techniques: A Handbook for Faculty.* San Francisco: Jossey-Bass.

Argyris, C. 1976. *Increasing Leadership Effectiveness.* New York: Wiley-Interscience.

Assad, Arjang A., and Judy D. Olian. 1995. "Total Quality and the Academy: Continuously Improving the University of Maryland." In *Academic Initiatives in Total Quality for Higher Education,* edited by Harry V. Roberts. Milwaukee: ASQC Quality Press.

Association of American Colleges. 1985. *Integrity in the College Curriculum: A Report to the Academic Community.* Washington, D.C.: Author.

Astin, Alexander. 1981. "Proposals for Change in College Admin-

istration." In *Maximizing Leadership Effectiveness,* edited by
Alexander Astin and Rita Scherrei. San Francisco: Jossey-Bass.

Atkinson, Philip E. 1990. *Creating Culture Change: The Key to
Successful Total Quality Management.* Bedford, Eng.: IFS Ltd.

Baker, Wayne E. April 1994. "The Paradox of Empowerment." *Chief
Executive:* 62–65.

Balderston, Frederick E. 1995. *Managing Today's University: Strategies for Viability, Change, and Excellence.* 2d ed. San Francisco:
Jossey-Bass.

Barker, Joel Arthur. 1992. *Paradigms: The Business of Discovering
the Future.* New York: Harper Business.

Bass, B.M. 1985. *Leadership and Performance beyond Expectations.*
New York: Free Press.

Bateman, George R., and Harry V. Roberts. 1993. "TQM for Professors and Students." Unpublished manuscript. Chicago: Univ.
of Chicago, Graduate School of Business. ED 384 319. 25 pp.
MF–01; PC–01.

Batten, Joe. May 1994. "A Total Quality Culture." *Management
Review:* 61.

Beckhard, Richard, and Wendy Prichard. 1992. *Changing the
Essence: The Art of Creating and Leading Fundamental Change
in Organizations.* San Francisco: Jossey-Bass.

Bennis, Warren G. 1983. "The Artform of Leadership." In *The
Executive Mind: New Insights on Managerial Thought and
Action,* edited by S. Srivastva and Associates. San Francisco:
Jossey-Bass.

Bensimon, Estella, and Anna Neumann. 1993. *Redesigning
Collegiate Leadership: Teams and Teamwork in Higher
Education.* Baltimore: Johns Hopkins Univ. Press.

Bergquist, William H. 1995. *Quality through Access, Access with
Quality.* San Francisco: Jossey-Bass.

Berry, Thomas H. 1991. *Managing the Total Quality Transformation.* New York: McGraw-Hill.

Birnbaum, Robert. 1988. *How Colleges Work: The Cybernetics of
Academic Organization and Leadership.* San Francisco: Jossey-
Bass.

————. 1992. *How Academic Leadership Works.* San Francisco:
Jossey-Bass.

Block, Peter. 1989. *The Empowered Manager: Positive Political Skills
at Work.* San Francisco: Jossey-Bass.

————. 1993. *Stewardship: Choosing Service over Self-Interest.* San
Francisco: Berrett-Koehler.

Boardman, Thomas J. 1994. "The Statistician Who Changed the

World: W. Edwards Deming, 1900–1993." *American Statistician* 48: 179–87.

Bok, Derek. July/August 1992. "Reclaiming the Public Trust." *Change* 24: 13–19.

Bolman, Lee G., and Terrence E. Deal. 1991. *Reframing Organizations*. San Francisco: Jossey-Bass.

Bonser, Charles F. 1992. "Total Quality Education." *Public Administration Review* 52(5): 504–12.

Bonstingl, John J. September 1993. "The Quality Movement: What's It Really About?" *Educational Leadership:* 66.

Boyer, E.L. 9 March 1994. "Creating the New American College." *Chronicle of Higher Education:* A48.

Brassard, Michael. 1989. *The Memory Jogger Plus: Featuring the Seven Management and Planning Tools*. Methuen, Mass.: GOAL/QPC.

Brown, Mark G., Darcy E. Hitchcock, and Marsha L. Willard. 1994. *Why TQM Fails and What to Do about It*. New York: Irwin Professional Publishing.

Burns, J.M. 1978. *Leadership*. New York: Harper & Row.

Byrne, John A. 20 December 1993. "The Horizontal Corporation." *Business Week:* 76–81.

Calek, Anne. 1995. "1995 Quality in Education Listing." *Quality Progress* 28: 27–77.

Carlzon, Jan. 1987. *Moments of Truth*. Cambridge, Mass.: Ballinger Publishing Co.

Carothers, Robert L., and Jayne Richmond. 1993. "Faculty as Customers: Hard Lessons for Administrators." In *Continuous Quality Improvement: Making the Transition to Education,* edited by Dean L. Hubbard. Maryville, Mo.: Prescott Publishing Co.

Carothers, Robert L., and Mary Lou Sevigny. 1993. "Classism and Quality." In *Pursuit of Quality in Higher Education,* edited by Deborah J. Teeter and G. Gregory Lozier. New Directions for Institutional Research No. 78. San Francisco: Jossey-Bass.

Carr, Clay. 1994. "Empowered Organizations, Empowering Leaders." *Training* 48(3): 39–44.

Chaffee, Ellen Earle, and Daniel Seymour. November/December 1991. "Quality Improvement with Trustee Involvement." *AGB Reports:* 14–18.

Chaffee, Ellen Earle, and Lawrence A. Sherr. 1992. *Quality: Transforming Postsecondary Education*. ASHE-ERIC Higher Education Report No. 3. Washington, D.C.: Association for the Study of Higher Education. ED 351 922. 145 pp. MF–01; PC–06.

Chaffee, Ellen E., and William G. Tierney. 1988. *Collegiate Culture and Leadership Strategies.* New York: Macmillan.

Champy, James. 20 February 1995. "Reengineering Management: The Mandate for New Leadership." *Industry Week:* 32–33+.

Chronicle of Higher Education. 1994. *The Almanac of Higher Education.* Chicago: Univ. of Chicago Press.

Coate, Edwin L. November 1990. "TQM on Campus." *NACUBO Business Officer:* 26–35.

————. 1991. "Implementing Total Quality in a University Setting." In *Total Quality Management in Higher Education,* edited by Lawrence A. Sherr and Deborah J. Teeter. New Directions for Higher Education No. 71. San Francisco: Jossey-Bass.

Cocheu, Ted. 1993. *Making Quality Happen: How Training Can Turn Strategy into Real Improvement.* San Francisco: Jossey-Bass.

Cohen, M.D., and J.G. March. 1984. "Leadership in an Organized Anarchy." In *Organization and Governance in Higher Education,* edited by Robert Birnbaum. Lexington, Mass.: Ginn.

Conger, J.A. 1989. "Leadership: The Art of Empowering Others." *Academy of Management Executives* 3(1): 17–24.

Cope, Robert G. 1987. *Opportunity from Strength: Strategic Planning Clarified with Case Examples.* ASHE-ERIC Higher Education Report No. 8. Washington, D.C.: Association for the Study of Higher Education. ED 296 694. 149 pp. MF–01; PC–06.

Cornesky, Robert, Sam McCool, Larry Byrnes, and Robert Weber. 1991. *Implementing Total Quality Management in Higher Education.* Madison, Wisc.: Magna Publications. ED 343 535. 154 pp. MF–01; PC not available EDRS.

Cornesky, Robert A., et al. 1992. *Using Deming to Improve Quality in Colleges and Universities.* Madison, Wisc.: Magna Publications. ED 354 838. 122 pp. MF–01; PC not available EDRS.

Corts, Thomas E. 1992. "Customers: You Can't Do without Them." In *Quality Quest in the Academic Process,* edited by John W. Harris and J. Mark Baggett. Methuen, Mass.: GOAL/QPC.

Covey, Stephen R. 1989. *The Seven Habits of Highly Effective People.* New York: Simon & Schuster.

————. 1991. *Principle Centered Leadership.* New York: Summit Books.

Crosby, Philip B. 1979. *Quality Is Free.* New York: McGraw-Hill.

————. 1992. *Completeness: Quality for the 21st Century.* New York: Penguin Books.

Cross, K. Patricia. 1994. "Involving Faculty in TQM." In *CQI 101: A First Reader for Higher Education.* Washington, D.C.: American Association for Higher Education.

Crouch, J. Michael. 1992. *An Ounce of Application Is Worth a Ton of Abstractions: A Practical Guide to Implementing Total Quality Management.* Greensboro, N.C.: Leads Corp. ED 350 963. 247 pp. MF–01; PC–10.

Davis, S.M. 1984. *Managing Corporate Culture.* Cambridge, Mass.: Ballinger.

Deal, Terrence E., and Wilham A. Jenkins. 1994. *Managing the Hidden Organization: Strategies for Empowering Your Behind-the-Scenes Employees.* New York: Warner Books.

Deal, Terrence E., and Allan A. Kennedy. 1982. *Corporate Cultures: The Rites and Rituals of Corporate Life.* Reading, Mass.: Addison-Wesley.

Dehne, George C. November/December 1995. "The Silver Bullet Syndrome." *AGB Trusteeship:* 13–17.

Deming, W. Edwards. 1986. *Out of the Crisis.* Cambridge, Mass.: MIT, Center for Advanced Engineering Study.

———. 1993. *The New Economics.* Cambridge, Mass.: MIT, Center for Advanced Engineering Study.

Denton, D. Keith. January/February 1995. "Creating a System for Continuous Improvement." *Business Horizons:* 16–21.

Dertouzos, Michael L., Richard K. Lester, and Robert M. Solow. 1989. *Made in America.* Cambridge, Mass.: MIT Press.

Dhiman, Satinder, and Daniel Seymour. 1996. "Five Tips for Quality Leaders." *Contemporary Education* 67(2): 75–78.

Dill, David D. 1992. "Quality by Design: Toward a Framework for Academic Quality Management." In *Higher Education: Handbook of Theory and Research,* Vol. 8, edited by J. Smart. New York: Agathon Press.

Dobyns, Lloyd, and Clare Crawford-Mason. 1991. *Quality or Else: The Revolution in World Business.* Boston: Houghton Mifflin.

Doyle, Michael, and David Straus. 1976. *How to Make Meetings Work.* New York: Jove Books.

Drucker, Peter F. 1967. *The Effective Executive.* New York: Harper & Row.

Dumaine, Brian. 7 May 1990. "Who Needs a Boss?" *Fortune:* 52–60.

———. 17 October 1994. "Mr. Learning Organization." *Fortune:* 147–57.

Ebel, Kenneth E. 1991. *Achieving Excellence in Business: A Practical Guide to the Total Quality Transformation Process.* Milwaukee: ASQC Quality Press, Marcel Dekker, Inc.

Education Commission of the States. 1986. *Transforming the State Role in Undergraduate Education: Time for a Different View.* Denver: Author.

Entner, Donald. 1993. "DCCC Takes the TQM Plunge . . . and Tells How." *Educational Record* 74(2): 28–34.

Evans, John P. 1992. *A Report of the Total Quality Leadership Steering Committee and Working Councils*. Cincinnati: John K. Howe Co.

Ewell, Peter T. 1991. "Assessment and TQM: In Search of Convergence." In *Total Quality Management in Higher Education*, edited by Lawrence A. Sherr and Deborah J. Teeter. New Directions for Higher Education No. 71. San Francisco: Jossey-Bass.

———. 1993. "Total Quality and Academic Practice: The Idea We've Been Waiting For?" *Change* 25(3): 49–55.

Feigenbaum, A.V. November 1956. "Total Quality Control." *Harvard Business Review:* 93–101.

Fincher, Cameron. 1991. *Assessment, Improvement, and Cooperation: The Challenge of Reform in Higher Education*. Athens: Univ. of Georgia, Institute of Higher Education. ED 338 118. 86 pp. MF–01; PC–04.

Fisher, James L. 1984. *Power of the Presidency*. New York: ACE/Macmillan.

———. 1993. "TQM: A Warning for Higher Education." *Educational Record* 74(2): 15–19.

Freed, Jann E., and Marie Klugman. 1996. "Lessons Learned from Campus Visits: The Quality Principles and Practices in Higher Education." Poster session at the AAHE Conference on Assessment and Quality, June 9–12, Washington, D.C.

Freed, Jann E., Marie Klugman, and Jonathan D. Fife. 1994. "Total Quality Management on Campus: Implementation, Experiences, and Observations." Paper presented at an annual meeting of the Association for the Study of Higher Education, November 10–13, Tucson, Arizona. ED 375 734. 24 pp. MF–01; PC–01.

———. 1995. "Leaders for Quality: Quality Leaders." Paper presented at the AAHE Conference on Assessment and Quality, June 11–14, Boston, Massachusetts.

Gabor, Andrea. 1990. *The Man Who Discovered Quality*. New York: Times Books.

Garvin, David A. 1988. *Managing Quality*. New York: Free Press.

Gitlow, Howard S., and Shelly J. Gitlow. 1987. *The Deming Guide to Quality and Competitive Position*. Englewood Cliffs, N.J.: Prentice-Hall.

Gitlow, Howard, Alan Oppenheim, and Rosa Oppenheim. 1995. *Quality Management: Tools and Methods for Improvement*. Burr Ridge, Ill.: Irwin.

GOAL/QPC. 1988. *The Memory Jogger: A Pocket Guide of Tools for*

Continuous Improvement. Methuen, Mass.: Author.

Gore, E.W., Jr. 1993. "Total Quality Management in Education." In *Continuous Quality Improvement: Making the Transition to Education,* edited by Dean L. Hubbard. Maryville, Mo.: Prescott Publishing Co.

Graham, Morris A., and Melvin J. LeBaron. 1994. *The Horizontal Revolution.* San Francisco: Jossey-Bass.

Greenleaf, R.K. 1977. *Servant Leadership: A Journey into the Nature of Legitimate Power and Greatness.* New York: Paulist Press.

Guido-DiBrito, F., and L.E. Nathan. 1995. "Underlying Worldviews of Leadership." Unpublished manuscript. Cedar Falls: Univ. of Northern Iowa.

Hansen, Lee W. 1993. "Bringing Total Quality Improvement into the College Classroom." *Higher Education* 25: 259–79.

Harrington, H.J. 1987. *The Improvement Process.* New York: McGraw-Hill.

Helton, B. Ray. 5 May 1993. "Empowerment and Training." *Quality Observer:* 5.

Hiam, Alexander. 1992. *Closing the Quality Gap.* Englewood Cliffs, N.J.: Prentice-Hall.

Hillenmeyer, Susan G. 1992. "How Quality Improvement Teams Work to Improve Processes in Departments and Administrative Units." In *Quality Quest in the Academic Process,* edited by John W. Harris and J. Mark Baggett. Methuen, Mass.: GOAL/QPC.

Hodgetts, Richard. 1993. "A Conversation with Geert Hofstede." *Organizational Dynamics* 21(4): 53–61.

Hodgetts, R.M., F. Luthans, and S.M. Lee. Spring 1994. "New Paradigm Organizations: From Quality to Learning to World Class." *Organizational Dynamics:* 5–19.

Hoffman, Allan M., and Daniel J. Julius. 1995. *Total Quality Management: Implications for Higher Education.* Maryville, Mo.: Prescott Publishing Co.

Hogg, Robert V., and Mary C. Hogg. 1993. "Total Quality Management in Higher Education: A Paradigm Shift." Unpublished manuscript. Iowa City: Univ. of Iowa.

Holpp, Lawrence. 1989. "Ten Reasons Why Total Quality Is Less Than Total." *Training* 26: 93–103.

Hopkins, L. Thomas. 1937. *Integration: Its Meaning and Application.* New York: Appleton-Century-Crofts.

Horine, Julie E., William A. Hailey, and Laura Rubach. 1993. "Shaping America's Future." *Quality Progress* 26(10): 41–60.

Howard, Robert. September/October 1990. "Values Make the Company: An Interview with Robert Haas." *Harvard Business*

Review: 133–44.

Hubbard, Dean L., ed. 1993. *Continuous Quality Improvement: Making the Transition to Education.* Maryville, Mo.: Prescott Publishing Co.

Huey, John. 23 September 1991. "Nothing Is Impossible." *Fortune:* 135–40.

———. 21 February 1994. "The New Post-Heroic Leadership." *Fortune:* 42–50.

Hull, William E. 1992. "The Quality Quest in Academia." In *Quality Quest in the Academic Process,* edited by John W. Harris and J. Mark Baggett. Methuen, Mass.: GOAL/QPC.

———. 1995. "The Quality Culture in Academia and Its Implementation at Samford University." Paper presented at the AAHE Annual Conference on Assessment and Quality, June 11–14, Boston, Massachusetts.

Hunsinger, Ronald N. 1992. "Total Quality Improvement in the Basic Sciences: A Retrospective Case Study." In *Quality Quest in the Academic Process,* edited by John W. Harris and J. Mark Baggett. Methuen, Mass.: GOAL/QPC.

Hyson, Ronald J. 1991. "Point Seven: Institute Leadership." In *Applying the Deming Method to Higher Education,* edited by Richard I. Miller. Washington, D.C.: College and Personnel Association.

Imai, Masaaki. 1986. *Kaizen: The Key to Japan's Competitive Success.* New York: Random House.

Ishikawa, Kaoru. 1985. *What Is Total Quality Control? The Japanese Way,* translated by David J. Lu. Englewood Cliffs, N.J.: Prentice-Hall.

Janis, Irving L. 1972. *Victims of Groupthink.* Boston: Houghton Mifflin.

Juran, Joseph M. 1988. *Juran on Planning for Quality.* New York: Free Press.

———. 1989. *Juran on Leadership for Quality.* New York: Free Press.

———. 1992. *Juran on Quality by Design: The New Steps for Planning Quality into Goods and Services.* New York: Free Press.

———. 1995a. *A History of Managing for Quality.* Milwaukee: ASQC Quality Press.

———. December 1995b. "A History of Managing for Quality in the United States." *Quality Digest:* 34–45.

Kanter, Rosabeth Moss. 1983. *The Change Masters.* New York: Simon & Schuster.

Katzenbach, Jon R., and Douglas K. Smith. 1993. *The Wisdom of Teams: Creating the High Performance Organization.* Boston: Harvard Business School Press.

Keller, George. 1983. *Academic Strategy: The Management Revolution in American Higher Education.* Baltimore: Johns Hopkins Univ. Press.

Kelly, Dennis. 20 February 1996. "Private Colleges Holding Down Tuition Increases." *USA Today:* 1.

Kerr, Clark. 1990. "Higher Education Cannot Escape History: The 1990s." In *An Agenda for the New Decade.* New Directions for Higher Education No. 70. San Francisco: Jossey-Bass.

Ketchum, Lyman D., and Eric Trist. 1992. *All Teams Are Not Created Equal: How Employee Empowerment Really Works.* Newbury Park, Calif.: Sage.

Kiefer, Charles F., and Peter M. Senge. 1986. *Metanoic Organizations: Experiments in Organizational Innovation.* Framingham, Mass.: Innovation Associates.

Kilmann, Ralph, Teresa Joyce Covin, and Associates. 1988. *Corporate Transformation: Revitalizing Organizations for a Competitive World.* San Francisco: Jossey-Bass.

Knauft, E.B., Renee A. Berger, and Sandra T. Gray. 1991. *Profiles of Excellence: Achieving Success in the Nonprofit Sector.* San Francisco: Jossey-Bass.

Kouzes, James M., and Barry Z. Posner. 1993. *Credibility: How Leaders Gain and Lose It, Why People Demand It.* San Francisco: Jossey-Bass.

Kramer, Gary L. October 1985. "Why Students Persist in College: A Categorical Analysis." *NACADA Journal* 5(2): 1–17.

Kuh, George D., and Elizabeth J. Whitt. 1988. *The Invisible Tapestry: Culture in American Colleges and Universities.* ASHE-ERIC Higher Education Report No. 1. Washington, D.C.: Association for the Study of Higher Education. ED 299 934. 144 pp. MF–01; PC–06.

Law, James E. 1993. "Leaping over the Pitfalls of TQM." *School Business Affairs* 59(6): 21+.

Lawler, Edward E., III. 1986. *High Involvement Management: Participative Strategies for Improving Organizational Performance.* San Francisco: Jossey-Bass.

———. 1992. *The Ultimate Advantage: Creating the High Involvement Organization.* San Francisco: Jossey-Bass.

Lee, Chris, and Ron Zemke. June 1993. "The Search for Spirit in the Workplace." *Training:* 21–28.

Leffel, Linda G., Jerald F. Robinson, Richard F. Harshberger, John D.

Krallman, and Robert B. Frary. 1991. "Assessing the Leadership Culture at Virginia Tech." In *Total Quality Management in Higher Education,* edited by Lawrence A. Sherr and Deborah J. Teeter. New Directions for Higher Education No. 71. San Francisco: Jossey-Bass.

Leslie, David, and E.K. Fretwell. 1996. *Wise Moves in Hard Times: Creating and Managing Resilient Colleges and Universities.* San Francisco: Jossey-Bass.

LeTarte, Clyde E. 1993. "Seven Tips for Implementing TQM: A CEO's View from the Trenches." *Community College Journal* 1: 17–21.

Levine, Arthur. 1990. "The Clock Is Ticking." *Change:* 4–5.

Levine, David I., and Laura D'Andrea Tyson. 1990. "Participation, Productivity, and the Firm's Environment." In *Paying for Productivity: A Look at the Evidence,* edited by Alan S. Blinder. Washington, D.C.: Brookings Institution.

Lewis, G.R., and D.H. Smith. 1994. *Total Quality in Higher Education.* Delray Beach, Fla.: St. Lucie Press.

Lovett, Clara. 1994. "Assessment, CQI, and Faculty Culture." In *CQI 101: A First Reader for Higher Education.* Washington, D.C.: American Association for Higher Education.

Lytle, Chris. June 1995. "People Problems? The Solution Is in the System." *Radio Ink* 5-18: 16.

McGregor, Douglas. 1967. *The Professional Manager.* New York: McGraw-Hill.

McPherson, M.S., M.O. Schapiro, and G.C. Winston. 1993. *Paying the Piper: Productivity, Incentives, and Financing in U.S. Higher Education.* Ann Arbor: Univ. of Michigan Press.

Maier, N.R.F. 1970. *Problem Solving and Creativity in Individuals and Groups.* Belmont, Calif.: Brooks-Cole.

Manz, Charles C., and Henry P. Sims. 1980. "Self-Management as a Substitute for Leadership: A Social Learning Theory Perspective." *Academy of Management Review* 5(3): 361–67.

Marchese, Ted. 1993. "TQM: A Time for Ideas." *Change* 25(3): 10–13.

———. 1994. "Quality for the Long Haul." *AAHE Bulletin* 46(9): 8–10.

Martin, Paula K. September 1992. "The Missing Piece of the Total Quality Puzzle." *Training:* 90.

May, D. Kevin. 1991. "Point Nine: Break Down Barriers between Departments." In *Applying the Deming Method to Higher Education,* edited by Richard I. Miller. Washington, D.C.: College and University Personnel Association.

Mayhew, Lewis B., Patrick J. Ford, and Dean L. Hubbard. 1990. *The Quest for Quality: The Challenge for Undergraduate Education in the 1990s.* San Francisco: Jossey-Bass.

Melissaratos, Aris, and Carl Arendt. April 1992. "TQM Can Address Higher Ed's Ills." *NACUBO Business Officer:* 32–35.

Miller, Richard I. 1990. *Major American Higher Education Issues and Challenges in the 1990s.* London: Jessica Kingsley Publishers.

————. 1991. *Applying the Deming Method to Higher Education.* Washington, D.C.: College and University Personnel Association. ED 333 805. 138 pp. MF–01; PC–06.

Mosteller, F. 1989. "The Muddiest Point in the Lecture as a Feedback Device." *On Teaching and Learning: Journal of the Harvard-Danforth Center* 3: 10–21.

Nanus, Burt. 1992. *Visionary Leadership: Creating a Compelling Sense of Direction for Your Organization.* San Francisco: Jossey-Bass.

National Governors Association. 1986. *Time for Results: The Governors' 1991 Report on Education.* Washington, D.C.: Author.

National Institute of Education, Study Group on the Conditions of Excellence in American Higher Education. 1984. *Involvement in Learning: Realizing the Potential of American Higher Education.* Washington, D.C.: U.S. Government Printing Office.

National Institute of Standards and Technology. 5 February 1996. "Study Finds 'Quality Stocks' Yield Big Payoff." *NIST Update.*

Neal, Judith A., and Cheryl L. Tromley. 1995. "From Incremental Change to Retrofit: Creating High-Performance Work Systems." *Academy of Management Executive* 9(1): 42–54.

Neave, Henry R. 1990. *The Deming Dimension.* Knoxville: SPC Press.

Nielsen, D.N. 1993. "A Deming Approach to Promotion and Tenure." Paper presented at an annual meeting of the American Society for Engineering Education, June 20–24, Urbana, Illinois.

Nordvall, Robert C. 1982. *The Process of Change in Higher Education Institutions.* AAHE-ERIC Higher Education Research Report No. 7. Washington, D.C.: American Association for Higher Education.

O'Brien, Kathleen A., William McEachern, and Elizabeth A. Luther. 1996. "Human Resources Development and Management: Helping People Grow." In *High Performing Colleges: The Malcolm Baldrige National Quality Award as a Framework for Improving Higher Education,* edited by Daniel Seymour. Vol. 1, Theory and Concepts. Maryville, Mo.: Prescott Publishing Co.

Omachonu, Vincent K., and Joel E. Ross. 1994. *Principles of Total Quality*. Delray Beach, Fla.: St. Lucie Press.

Pascarella, Perry, and Mark A. Frohman. 1990. *The Purpose-Driven Organization: Unleashing the Power of Direction and Commitment*. San Francisco: Jossey-Bass.

Paulsen, Michael B. 1990. *College Choice: Understanding Student Enrollment Behavior*. ASHE-ERIC Higher Education Report No. 6. Washington, D.C.: George Washington Univ., Graduate School of Education and Human Development. ED 333 855. 121 pp. MF–01; PC–05.

Peachy, Burt, and Daniel Seymour. 1993. "Voice of the Customer: Using QFD as a Strategic Planning Tool." In *Continuous Quality Improvement: Making the Transition to Education,* edited by Dean L. Hubbard. Maryville, Mo.: Prescott Publishing Co.

Peters, Tom. 1987. *Thriving on Chaos*. New York: Harper Collins.

Pfeffer, Jeffrey. 1995. "Producing Sustainable Competitive Advantage through the Effective Management of People." *Academy of Management Executive* 9(1): 55–69.

Plsek, Paul E. 1990. "A Primer on Quality Improvement Tools." In *Curing Health Care,* edited by Donald M. Berwick, A. Blanton Godfrey, and Jane Roessner. San Francisco: Jossey-Bass.

Porras, Jerry I., and James C. Collins. 1994. *Built to Last: Successful Habits of Visionary Companies*. New York: Harper Collins.

Reynolds, Gary L. 1992. "Total Quality Management for Campus Facilities." *Facilities Manager:* 14–20.

Rice, R.E., and A.E. Austin. 1988. "High Faculty Morale: What Exemplary Colleges Do Right." *Change* 20(2): 51–58.

Roberts, Harry V., ed. 1995. *Academic Initiatives in Total Quality for Higher Education*. Milwaukee: ASQC Quality Press.

Robinson, J.D., H.A. Poling, J.F. Akers, E.L. Artzt, and P.A. Allaire. November/December 1991. "An Open Letter: TQM on the Campus." *Harvard Business Review:* 94–95.

Ross, Joel E. 1993. *Total Quality Management: Text, Cases, and Readings*. Delray Beach, Fla.: St. Lucie Press.

Ruben, Brent D. 1995a. "Defining and Assessing 'Quality' in Higher Education." In *Quality in Higher Education,* edited by Brent D. Ruben. New Brunswick, N.J.: Transaction Publishers.

———. 1995b. "The Quality Approach in Higher Education: Context and Concepts for Change." In *Quality in Higher Education,* edited by Brent D. Ruben. New Brunswick, N.J.: Transaction Publishers.

Russell, Peter, and Roger Evans. 1992. *The Creative Manager: Finding Inner Vision and Wisdom in Uncertain Times*. San

Francisco: Jossey-Bass.

Ryan, Kathleen D., and Daniel K. Oestreich. 1991. *Driving Fear Out of the Workplace*. San Francisco: Jossey-Bass.

Sashkin, Marshall, and Kenneth J. Kiser. 1993. *Putting Total Quality Management to Work*. San Francisco: Berrett-Koehler.

Schein, E.H. Summer 1983. "The Role of the Founder in Creating Organizational Culture." *Organizational Dynamics* 12: 13–28.

———. 1985. *Organizational Culture and Leadership*. San Francisco: Jossey-Bass.

Schmidt, Warren H., and Jerome P. Finnigan. 1992. *The Race without a Finish Line*. San Francisco: Jossey-Bass.

———. 1993. *TQManager: A Practical Guide for Managing in a Total Quality Organization*. San Francisco: Jossey-Bass.

Scholtes, Peter R. 1988. *The Team Handbook: How to Use Teams to Improve Quality*. Madison, Wisc.: Joiner Associates.

———. 1994. *The Team Handbook for Educators: How to Use Teams to Improve Quality*. Madison, Wisc.: Joiner Associates.

Schwartz, H., and S.M. Davis. Summer 1981. "Matching Corporate Culture and Business Strategy." *Organizational Dynamics* 10(1): 30–48.

Seagren, Alan T., John W. Creswell, and Daniel W. Wheeler. 1993. *The Department Chair: New Roles, Responsibilities, and Challenges*. ASHE-ERIC Higher Education Report No. 1. Washington, D.C.: George Washington Univ., Graduate School of Education and Human Development. ED 363 164. 129 pp. MF–01; PC–06.

Senge, Peter M. 1990. *The Fifth Discipline*. New York: Doubleday/Currency.

Serritella, Vince. 1995. "Quality at Motorola." Paper presented at the Midwest Business Administration Association, March, Chicago, Illinois.

Seymour, Daniel T. November 1991. "TQM on Campus: What the Pioneers Are Finding." *AAHE Bulletin* 44(3): 10–13.

———. 1992. *On Q: Causing Quality in Higher Education*. Phoenix, Ariz.: American Council on Education/Oryx Press.

———. 1993a. *Total Quality Management in Higher Education: Clearing the Hurdles*. No. 93-101. Methuen, Mass.: GOAL/QPC.

———. 1993b. "TQM: Focus on Performance, Not Resources." *Educational Record* 74(2): 6–14.

———. 1995. *Once Upon a Campus*. Phoenix, Ariz.: American Council on Education/Oryx Press.

———, ed. 1996. *High Performing Colleges: The Malcolm Baldrige National Quality Award as a Framework for Improving Higher Education*. Maryville, Mo.: Prescott Publishing Co.

Seymour, Daniel, and Casey Collett. 1991. *Total Quality Management in Higher Education: A Critical Assessment.* Methuen, Mass.: GOAL/QPC.

Sherr, Lawrence A., and G. Gregory Lozier. 1991. "Total Quality Management in Higher Education." In *Total Quality Management in Higher Education,* edited by Lawrence A. Sherr and Deborah J. Teeter. New Directions for Higher Education No. 71. San Francisco: Jossey-Bass.

Sherr, Lawrence A., and Deborah J. Teeter. 1991. *Total Quality Management in Higher Education.* New Directions for Higher Education No. 71. San Francisco: Jossey-Bass.

Shulman, Gary M., and David L. Luechauer. 1993. "The Empowering Education: A CQI Approach to Classroom Leadership." In *Continuous Quality Improvement: Making the Transition to Education,* edited by Dean L. Hubbard. Maryville, Mo.: Prescott Publishing Co.

Simon, Hermann. 1996. *Hidden Champions: Lessons from 500 of the World's Best Unknown Companies.* Boston: Harvard Business School Press.

Smircich, L. 1983. "Concepts of Culture and Organizational Analysis." *Administrative Science Quarterly* 28: 339–58.

Smith, P. 1990. *Killing the Spirit.* New York: Penguin Books.

Spanbauer, Stanley J. 1992. *A Quality System for Education.* Milwaukee: ASQC Quality Press.

Steeples, Marion M. 1992. *The Corporate Guide to the Malcolm Baldrige National Quality Award.* Milwaukee: ASQC Quality Press.

Strickland, Billy J., and Shirley A. Schooley. 1993. *Quality Manual for Improving Academic Processes.* Birmingham, Ala.: Samford Univ.

Sykes, Charles J. 1988. *ProfScam: Professors and the Demise of Higher Education.* New York: St. Martin's Press.

Tague, Nancy R. 1995. *The Quality Toolbox.* Milwaukee: ASQC Quality Press.

Teal, Janice R. 1992. "Fear in the Classroom: Implications for Quality Improvement." In *Quality Quest in the Academic Process,* edited by John W. Harris and J. Mark Baggett. Methuen, Mass.: GOAL/QPC.

Thomson, Suzanne B., and Charlotte M. Roberts. July/August 1992. "Leading Total Quality." *Journal for Quality and Participation:* 46–52.

Thor, Linda M. 1993. "The Human Side of Quality: Employee Care and Empowerment." Paper presented at a conference of the

League for Innovation in the Community College, "Community Colleges and Corporations: Partners in Total Quality Management," Irvine, California.

———. 1995. "First among Teammates. Creating Collective Power Leadership: The Driver of the System." Unpublished manuscript. Phoenix: Rio Salado Community College.

———. 1996. "Leadership: The Driver of the System." In *High Performing Colleges,* vol. 1, edited by Daniel Seymour. Maryville, Mo.: Prescott Publishing Co.

Tice, Lou. 2 May 1993. "Why TQM Doesn't Work." *Quality Observer:* 19–20.

Tichy, N.M., and M.A. Devanna. 1986. *The Transformational Leader.* New York: Wiley.

"To Dance with Change." 1994. *Policy Perspectives* 5(3): A1–12.

"Transatlantic Dialogue." 1993. *Policy Perspectives* 5(1): A1–11.

Tucker, Shirley. 1993. "Human Resources Improvement at the University of Pittsburgh." In *Continuous Quality Improvement: Making the Transition to Education,* edited by Dean L. Hubbard. Maryville, Mo.: Prescott Publishing Co.

U.S. Department of Education, National Center for Education Statistics. 1995. *The Condition of Education.* Washington, D.C.: U.S. GPO.

VanDyke, Patt, ed. 1995. *The Culture for Quality.* Maryville, Mo.: Prescott Publishing Co.

Vroom, V.H., and P.W. Yetton. 1973. *Leadership and Decision Making.* Pittsburgh: Univ. of Pittsburgh Press.

Wadsworth, Harrison M., Kenneth S. Stephens, and A. Blanton Godfrey. 1986. *Modern Methods for Quality Control and Improvement.* New York: Wiley.

Walton, Mary. 1986. *The Deming Management Method.* New York: Perigee Books.

———. 1990. *Deming Management at Work.* New York: G.P. Putnam's Sons.

Waterman, Robert H. 1987. *The Renewal Factor.* New York: Bantam Books.

Weinstein, L.A. 1993. *Moving a Battleship with Your Bare Hands: Governing a University System.* Madison, Wisc.: Magna Publications. ED 362 114. 302 pp. MF–01; PC not available EDRS.

Wellins, Richard S., William Byham, and Jeanne M. Wilson. 1991. *Empowered Teams.* San Francisco: Jossey-Bass.

Wheatley, Margaret J. 1994. *Leadership and the New Science: Learning about Organization from an Orderly Universe.* San Francisco: Berrett-Koehler.

Whetten, David A., and Kim S. Cameron. 1985. "Administrative Effectiveness in Higher Education." *Review of Higher Education* 9(1): 35–49.

Whiteley, Richard C. 1991. *The Customer-Driven Company: Moving Talk to Action*. Reading, Mass.: Addison-Wesley.

Wilshire, B. 1990. *The Moral Collapse of the University: Professionalism, Purity, and Alienation*. Albany: State Univ. of New York Press.

Wingspread Group on Higher Education. 1993. *An American Imperative: Higher Expectations for Higher Education*. Racine, Wisc.: Johnson Foundation.

Winter, Robert S. 1991. "Overcoming Barriers to Total Quality Management in Colleges and Universities." In *Total Quality Management in Higher Education,* edited by Lawrence A. Sherr and Deborah J. Teeter. New Directions for Higher Education No. 71. San Francisco: Jossey-Bass.

Winter, Robert S., and Elizabeth S. Winter. 1993. "Team Effectiveness." In *Continuous Quality Improvement,* edited by Dean L. Hubbard. Maryville, Mo.: Prescott Publishing Co.

Wolverton, Mimi. 1993. "Total Quality Management in Higher Education: Latest Fad or Lasting Legacy?" Policy Briefs of the Education Policy Studies Laboratory No. 93-101. Tempe: Arizona State Univ.

———. 1994. *A New Alliance: Continuous Quality and Classroom Effectiveness*. ASHE-ERIC Higher Education Report No. 6. Washington, D.C.: George Washington Univ., Graduate School of Education and Human Development. ED 392 369. 100 pp. MF–01; PC–04.

INDEX

current member of the Academic Quality Consortium, 30
    among the first to adopt the Quality Principles, 15
Baldrige winners' common stock increases in value of, 14
Belmont University in Nashville
    among the first to adopt the Quality Principles, 15
    current member of the Academic Quality Consortium, 30
    customer/supplier triad of, 60-61
Bergquist's definition of quality, 25
boundary-less companies, 106
brainstorming session
    tool to bring structure to, 97
Brazosport College
    among the first to adopt the Quality Principles, 15
breaking down barriers among organizational units
    as aspect of academic leadership, 135
Brigham, Steve
    thanks for input in design of survey instrument, xv
building a shared vision, 131-132
building trust so that assumptions can be challenged
    as aspect of academic leadership, 136

C

campus
    committees typically function as groups of individuals, 111
    Quality Coordinators Network, 30
cause analysis tools, 88-89
Cause-and-Effect Diagram, 96-98
    for Causes of Fear in the Classroom, 94, 97
    for Declining Summer School Enrollments, 97-98
Causes of Fear in Classroom as cause-and-Effect Diagram, 94, 97
Central College, financial assistance of, xv
Central Connecticut State University
    among the first to adopt the Quality Principles, 15
change as a positive and continuous in institutional culture, 118
classroom assessment techniques strengths, 33
Clemson University
    current member of the Academic Quality Consortium, 30
    among the first to adopt the Quality Principles, 15
collaboration, 111-118
    and teamwork need, 47
    as a quality principle, 11
college
    costs continuing rise, 4

effective leaders, 55, 134

El Camino Community College

    among the first to adopt the Quality Principles, 15

employees

    in a quality culture, 42-43

    involvement requirements, 106

    involvement theory, 20

    support insufficient as a mistake in implementation, 138-139

employers

    as important assessors of the results of education process, 33

empowered culture

    first step in creating, 55

empowered employees

    needs of, 107

empowering

    environment value, 107

    managers redefine and share powers and responsibilities, 104

    rather than controlling leadership important, 129

empowerment practice at root of organizational effectiveness, 104

evaluation tools, 88-89

exemplary presidents, 128

external stakeholders in academic institutions, 62

F

facilitators, 115

failed presidents, 127

fairness important for a quality culture, 107

Federal Express Corp., 20, 109

    winner of the Malcolm Baldrige Quality Award, 22

"felt need" necessary for change is, 53

fishbone diagram. See Cause-and-Effect Diagram

flow charts, 90-93

    of the Payroll Process, 90-91

    picture of separate steps of a process in sequential order, 90

Fordham University

    among the first to adopt the Quality Principles, 15

formal compliance, 130

Fox Valley Technical College

    among the first to adopt the Quality Principles, 15

one of first institutions involved in quality movement, 28
fundamental change in education
> forced by financial pressures and technological progress, 6

G

gaffs in implementation, xii
General Motors - Cadillac Division
> winner of the Malcolm Baldrige Quality Award, 22

genuine compliance, 130
George Mason University
> among the first to adopt the Quality Principles, 15

The George Washington University financial assistance, xv
Georgia Institute of Technology
> current member of the Academic Quality Consortium, 30

> among the first to adopt the Quality Principles, 15

Globe Metallurgical, Inc.
> winner of the Malcolm Baldrige Quality Award, 22

Graduate Record Examination
> verbal score has not recovered from the decline of 1960s, 4

Grand Rapids Junior College
> among the first to adopt the Quality Principles, 15

Granite Rock Co. winner of the Malcolm Baldrige Quality Award,
> 22

GRE. See Graduate Record Examination
group dynamics, 20
"groupthink," 118
grudging compliance, 130
GTE Directories winner of the Malcolm Baldrige Quality Award, 22
guiding questions make meetings more effective and efficient, 116

H

Haas, Robert
> empowerment is not easy, 105

Hewlett-Packard, 20
higher education
> authors that support the concept of an education
> > system based on the quality principles, 14

> changes in the past, 52-53

> criteria to define quality, 24-25

> current culture is often at odds with historic values of, 1

> historically evaluated itself on inputs, 10

> institutions not committed for the long term, 140

> need for change, 10

historical practices as obstacles to continuous improvement, 5-6
Houghton, Jamie, 118

I

IBM Rochester winner of the Malcolm Baldrige Quality Award, 22
idea creation tools, 88-89, 98
individual development systematic and continuous, 46
inputs as a higher education criteria to define quality, 24
Institutional
      Leadership Project findings, 127
      reputation definition for two decades after World War II, 1
      sources of opportunity preserved and highlighted, 127
      success depends upon how well people relate to each
      other, 65
      vision need to incorporate into daily activities, 54
institutions
      past criteria of quality of, 57
      reluctance to pay costs as a mistake in implementation, 140
      that are very successful exceed stakeholders' expectations,
      57
Integrity in the College Curriculum, 32
Intel, 20
interaction importance, 68
internal
      common language necessary for effective communication, 82
      stakeholders in academic institutions, 62
"invisible tapestry" of culture, 35
Involvement in Learning, 32
Ishikawa, Kaoru, 97
      quality control circles as contribution of, 18
Ishikawa diagram. See Cause-and-Effect Diagram

J

Japan
      quality improvement taught by Deming in, 17, 86
Japanese
      Federation of Economic Organizations, 17
      strategies to produce quality revolution, 18
Juran, Joseph M.
      applied Pareto principle to problems involving quality, 100-
      101
      conducted training courses in Japan, 17
      ideas on quality management, 19

among the first to adopt the Quality Principles, 15
Marietta College
    current member of the Academic Quality Consortium, 30
    among the first to adopt the Quality Principles, 15
marketing of institution is highest priority for colleges, 2
Marlow Industries winner of the Malcolm Baldrige Quality Award,
    22
Massy, Bill
    people doubt higher education has value for money, 5
"Mental models" as an analogy to explain a paradigm shift, 51-52
Miami University
    current member of the Academic Quality Consortium, 30
middle managers need power and accountability, 106
Miliken & Co., 20
    winner of the Malcolm Baldrige Quality Award, 22
mimicked catchphrases, xii
mismatch between what American society needs and what is
    receiving in higher education, 2
mission statement outlines purpose, 55
modal presidents, 127
moment of truth, 59
motivation through achievement, 20
Motorola, Inc., 20
    spending money on education and training because higher
        education system not working for it, 5
    winner of the Malcolm Baldrige Quality Award, 22
Motorola University
    trains employees so understand how affect stakeholders, 59

N

NACUBO. See National Association of College and University
    Business Officers
National Association of College and University Business Officers, 31
national index of public support, 4
new cultures are needed to support necessary changes, 8
new leadership theory, 20
Nominal Group Process as a method for group brainstorming, 98
Non-compliance, 130
Nordstrom rule # 1, 104
Northwest Missouri State University
    current member of the Academic Quality Consortium, 30
    early decision to embrace quality principles of, 15, 28, 144
nurture the support of strategic constituencies, 126

O

open systems, 68
Oregon State University
      current member of the Academic Quality Consortium, 30
      among the first to adopt the Quality Principles, 15, 28
organizational development, 20
organizations structured around functions, 117
outputs as a higher education criteria to define quality, 24-25
overcommunication better, especially during times of flux, 126-127

P

paradigm, 51
      shifting, 51-54
Pareto Diagram, 100-102
      examples, 99, 100
participative decision making when appropriate, 106
Payroll Process Flow Chart, 90-91
Pennsylvania State University
      among the first to adopt the Quality Principles, 15
      current member of the Academic Quality Consortium, 30
person-focused to system-focused thinking conceptual shift, 141
philosophy of quality as a post-World War II phenomenon, 17
place equal emphasis on process and outcomes, 125-126
Plan-Do-Check-Act cycle, 86
Planning for change, 47, 119-121
      as a quality principle, 11-12
planning tools, 88-89
practice, 12
principles, 12, 44
"process"
      analysis tools, 88-89
      as a concept in understanding systems, 68-69
      -based assessment approach involves three steps, 32-33
public trust loss
      due to lack of evidence of impact of higher education, 3
purpose of monograph, 5

Q

QFD. See Quality Function Deployment
Quality, 23-25
      as something people do rather than a state of being, 24
      assessment and improvement process, 139
      awards issued by states, 7

ASHE-ERIC HIGHER EDUCATION REPORTS

Since 1983, the Association for the Study of Higher Education (ASHE) and the Educational Resources Information Center (ERIC) Clearinghouse on Higher Education, a sponsored project of the Graduate School of Education and Human Development at The George Washington University, have cosponsored the ASHE-ERIC Higher Education Report series. This volume is the twenty-fifth overall and the eighth to be published by the Graduate School of Education and Human Development at The George Washington University.

Each monograph is the definitive analysis of a tough higher education problem, based on thorough research of pertinent literature and institutional experiences. Topics are identified by a national survey. Noted practitioners and scholars are then commissioned to write the reports, with experts providing critical reviews of each manuscript before publication.

Eight monographs (10 before 1985) in the ASHE-ERIC Higher Education Report series are published each year and are available on individual and subscription bases. To order, use the order form on the last page of this book.

Qualified persons interested in writing a monograph for the ASHE-ERIC Higher Education Report series are invited to submit a proposal to the National Advisory Board. As the preeminent literature review and issue analysis series in higher education, the Higher Education Reports are guaranteed wide dissemination and national exposure for accepted candidates. Execution of a monograph requires at least a minimal familiarity with the ERIC database, including *Resources in Education* and the current *Index to Journals in Education*. The objective of these reports is to bridge conventional wisdom with practical research. Prospective authors are strongly encouraged to call Dr. Fife at 800-773-3742.

For further information, write to
ASHE-ERIC Higher Education Reports
The George Washington University
One Dupont Circle, Suite 630
Washington, DC 20036
Or phone (202) 296-2597; toll free: 800-773-ERIC.

Write or call for a complete catalog.

Visit our web site at http://www.gwu.edu/~eriche

ADVISORY BOARD

James Earl Davis
University of Delaware at Newark

Cassie Freeman
Peabody College–Vanderbilt University

Susan Frost
Emory University

Mildred Garcia
Arizona State University West

James Hearn
University of Georgia

Philo Hutcheson
Georgia State University

CONSULTING EDITORS

Philip G. Altbach
State University of New York–Buffalo

Marilyn J. Amey
University of Kansas

Thomas A. Angelo
AAHE Assessment Forum

Louis C. Attinasi
Loyola University

Robert Boice
State University of New York–Stony Brook

Steve Brigham
American Association for Higher Education

Ivy E. Broder
The American University

Robert A. Cornesky
Cornesky and Associates, Inc.

Barbara Gross Davis
University of California at Berkeley

James R. Davis
Center for Academic Quality and Assessment of Student
    Learning

Cheryl Falk
Yakima Valley Community College

L. Dee Fink
University of Oklahoma

Anne H. Frank
American Association of University Professors

Joseph E. Gilmore
Northwest Missouri State University

Dean L. Hubbard
Northwest Missouri State University

Mardee Jenrette
Miami-Dade Community College

George D. Kuh
Indiana University

Robert Menges
Northwestern University

Diane E. Morrison
Centre for Curriculum and Professional Development

L. Jackson Newell
University of Utah

Steven G. Olswang
University of Washington

Brent Ruben
State University of New Jersey–Rutgers

Sherry Sayles-Folks
Eastern Michigan University

Daniel Seymour
Claremont College–California

Pamela D. Sherer
The Center for Teaching Excellence

Marilla D. Svinicki
University of Texas–Austin

David Sweet
OERI, U.S. Department of Education

Kathe Taylor
State of Washington Higher Education Coordinating Board

Gershon Vincow
Syracuse University

W. Allan Wright
Dalhousie University

Donald H. Wulff
University of Washington

Manta Yorke
Liverpool John Moores University

REVIEW PANEL

Charles Adams
University of Massachusetts–Amherst

Louis Albert
American Association for Higher Education

Richard Alfred
University of Michigan

Henry Lee Allen
University of Rochester

Philip G. Altbach
Boston College

Marilyn J. Amey
University of Kansas

Kristine L. Anderson
Florida Atlantic University

Karen D. Arnold
Boston College

Robert J. Barak
Iowa State Board of Regents

Alan Bayer
Virginia Polytechnic Institute and State University

John P. Bean
Indiana University–Bloomington

John M. Braxton
Peabody College, Vanderbilt University

Ellen M. Brier
Tennessee State University

Barbara E. Brittingham
The University of Rhode Island

Dennis Brown
University of Kansas

Peter McE. Buchanan
Council for Advancement and Support of Education

Patricia Carter
University of Michigan

John A. Centra
Syracuse University

Arthur W. Chickering
George Mason University

Darrel A. Clowes
Virginia Polytechnic Institute and State University

Cynthia S. Dickens
Mississippi State University

Deborah M. DiCroce
Piedmont Virginia Community College

Sarah M. Dinham
University of Arizona

Kenneth A. Feldman
State University of New York–Stony Brook

Dorothy E. Finnegan
The College of William & Mary

Mildred Garcia
Montclair State College

Rodolfo Z. Garcia
Commission on Institutions of Higher Education

Kenneth C. Green
University of Southern California

James Hearn
University of Georgia

Edward R. Hines
Illinois State University

Deborah Hunter
University of Vermont

Philo Hutcheson
Georgia State University

Bruce Anthony Jones
University of Pittsburgh

Elizabeth A. Jones
The Pennsylvania State University

Kathryn Kretschmer
University of Kansas

Marsha V. Krotseng
State College and University Systems of West Virginia

George D. Kuh
Indiana University–Bloomington

Daniel T. Layzell
University of Wisconsin System

Patrick G. Love
Kent State University

Cheryl D. Lovell
State Higher Education Executive Officers

Meredith Jane Ludwig
American Association of State Colleges and Universities

Dewayne Matthews
Western Interstate Commission for Higher Education

Mantha V. Mehallis
Florida Atlantic University

Toby Milton
Essex Community College

James R. Mingle
State Higher Education Executive Officers

John A. Muffo
Virginia Polytechnic Institute and State University

L. Jackson Newell
Deep Springs College

James C. Palmer
Illinois State University

Robert A. Rhoads
The Pennsylvania State University

G. Jeremiah Ryan
Harford Community College

Mary Ann Danowitz Sagaria
The Ohio State University

Daryl G. Smith
The Claremont Graduate School

William G. Tierney
University of Southern California

Susan B. Twombly
University of Kansas

Robert A. Walhaus
University of Illinois–Chicago

Harold Wechsler
University of Rochester

Elizabeth J. Whitt
University of Illinois–Chicago

Michael J. Worth
The George Washington University

RECENT TITLES

Volume 24 ASHE-ERIC Higher Education Reports

1. Tenure, Promotion, and Reappointment: Legal and Administrative Implications (951)
   Benjamin Baez and John A. Centra

2. Taking Teaching Seriously: Meeting the Challenge of Instructional Improvement (952)
   Michael B. Paulsen and Kenneth A. Feldman

3. Empowering the Faculty: Mentoring Redirected and Renewed (953)
   Gaye Luna and Deborah L. Cullen

4. Enhancing Student Learning: Intellectual, Social, and Emotional Integration (954)
   Anne Goodsell Love and Patrick G. Love

5. Benchmarking in Higher Education: Adapting Best Practices to Improve Quality (955)
   Jeffrey W. Alstete

6. Models for Improving College Teaching: A Faculty Resource (956)
   Jon E. Travis

7. Experiential Learning in Higher Education: Linking Classroom and Community (957)
   Jeffrey A. Cantor

8. Successful Faculty Development and Evaluation: The Complete Teaching Portfolio (958)
   John P. Murray

Volume 23 ASHE-ERIC Higher Education Reports

1. The Advisory Committee Advantage: Creating an Effective Strategy for Programmatic Improvement (941)
   Lee Teitel

2. Collaborative Peer Review: The Role of Faculty in Improving College Teaching (942)
   Larry Keig and Michael D. Waggoner

3. Prices, Productivity, and Investment: Assessing Financial Strategies in Higher Education (943)
   Edward P. St. John

4. The Development Officer in Higher Education: Toward an Understanding of the Role (944)
   Michael J. Worth and James W. Asp II

5. Measuring Up: The Promises and Pitfalls of Performance Indicators in Higher Education (945)
   Gerald Gaither, Brian P. Nedwek, and John E. Neal

Volume 21 ASHE-ERIC Higher Education Reports

1. The Leadership Compass: Values and Ethics in Higher Education (921)
   John R. Wilcox and Susan L. Ebbs

2. Preparing for a Global Community: Achieving an International Perspective in Higher Education (922)
   Sarah M. Pickert

3. Quality: Transforming Postsecondary Education (923)
   Ellen Earle Chaffee and Lawrence A. Sherr

4. Faculty Job Satisfaction: Women and Minorities in Peril (924)
   Martha Wingard Tack and Carol Logan Patitu

5. Reconciling Rights and Responsibilities of Colleges and Students: Offensive Speech, Assembly, Drug Testing, and Safety (925)
   Annette Gibbs

6. Creating Distinctiveness: Lessons from Uncommon Colleges and Universities (926)
   Barbara K. Townsend, L. Jackson Newell, and Michael D. Wiese

7. Instituting Enduring Innovations: Achieving Continuity of Change in Higher Education (927)
   Barbara K. Curry

8. Crossing Pedagogical Oceans: International Teaching Assistants in U.S. Undergraduate Education (928)
   Rosslyn M. Smith, Patricia Byrd, Gayle L. Nelson, Ralph Pat Barrett, and Janet C. Constantinides

ORDER FORM

Quantity   **Amount**

_____ Please begin my subscription to the current year's *ASHE-ERIC Higher Education Reports* (Volume 25) at $120.00, over 33% off the cover price, starting with Report 1.   _____

_____ Please send a complete set of Volume ___ *ASHE-ERIC Higher Education Reports* at $120.00, over 33% off the cover price.   _____

Individual reports are available for $24.00 and include the cost of shipping and handling.

SHIPPING POLICY:

- Books are sent UPS Ground or equivalent. For faster delivery, call for charges.
- Alaska, Hawaii, U.S. Territories and Foreign Countries, please call for shipping information.
- Order will be shipped within 24 hours after receipt of request.
- Orders of 10 or more books, call for shipping information.

All prices shown are subject to change.

Returns: No cash refunds—credit will be applied to future orders.

PLEASE SEND ME THE FOLLOWING REPORTS:

Quantity	Volume/No.	Title	Amount

Please check one of the following:

☐ Check enclosed, payable to GWU-ERIC.   **Subtotal:** _____

☐ Purchase order attached.   **Less Discount:** _____

☐ Charge my credit card indicated below:

   ☐ Visa   ☐ MasterCard   **Total Due:** _____

Expiration Date_____

Name_____

Title_____

Institution_____

Address_____

City _____ State _____ Zip_____

Phone _____ Fax _____ Telex_____

Signature _____ Date_____

SEND ALL ORDERS TO: ASHE-ERIC Higher Education Reports
The George Washington University
One Dupont Cir., Ste. 630, Washington, DC 20036-1183
Phone: (202) 296-2597 • Toll-free: 800-773-ERIC
FAX: (202) 452-1844
http://www.gwu.edu/~eriche